HOOK
REMEMBERED
again

Woolworth's and Homeware, Hook, 1960

Hook Road and Vale Terrace c1935

S O overwhelming was the response to the Remembered Series of books on the local history of Hook, Chessington, Tolworth and Long Ditton that people often asked: When is the next book coming out? The author's postbag has been full of letters from readers recounting tales from the past and some have included rare and unpublished photographs. Here, some new memories of the bygone rural days of Hook, Southborough and Surbiton are shared for the first time. Also revealed exclusively is the precise location of author Thomas Hardy's home in the Hook Road. It was here he was living in 1874 when the book Far From The Madding Crowd was first published. The author and fellow researcher Colin Prendergast have delved deep into the misty past to establish where Hardy and his wife lived during this important milestone in the writer's life. Until now, the location of Hardy's home in the old parish of Hook has been enshrouded in mystery and not even a visiting expert from the States had been able to make the discovery. Nostalgic recollections of life in some of the old village's vanished villas are also related, illustrated with some striking new period photographs and memorabilia.

———————◆———————

Acknowledgments

Colin Prendergast, Dennis Stickley, Viv Winstone, David Tippett-Wilson, Richard Skelton, Wendy Smith, Evelyn Pryor, Marion and George Bone, Elizabeth Fraser and family, Ron Hook, Joyce Morris, Martin Draper, Bob Cook, Roy Dack, Ray Cook, Garth and Ingrid Holford, Geoffrey Mellalieu, Reg Driver, Bill and Gillian Aldred, Bob Sewell, Les Eede, Pam Neame, Eileen Robinson, Fred Wilgoss, Peter Forsdick, Christine Wright, Elaine Barron, Maureen Smith, Vi Goddard, Eileen Gould, Fred Thompson, William Farmer, Rev Eric Heather, Rev John Balcom, Norman Newling, Peter Ketteringham, Gwendolen Freeman, Michael de Carle, John Oborn, P Muggleton, Lilian Swindall, Betty Odell, Mr and Mrs C Denham, Carol and Jeff Benn, Diana and Ken Hill, Doreen Conroy, Violet Goldsack, Pam Sillence, Peter Bridge, Gay Taylor, Jill Lamb, Rev Canon B. Mountford, Nigel Davison, John and Joyce Finch, Paul Adams, John Last, Anne Condello, Alison Morris, P Sparks, S. Veryard and Honeywell family, F Danilewicz, Winnie Randall, John Randall, staff of Oxford Central Library, Guildhall Library, Kingston Heritage Centre, Family History Centre, Hastings central library, Durham University library, Peter Butler, Mrs Hayllar, Surrey History Centre, June Sampson, Cambs Local Studies library, Balliol and Oriel Colleges, Martin Brebnor, Ron and Nora Ireland, M and N Davison, Danny Chisholm, Christine Wright, family of late Harry Ash, Alan Buller, Sheila Prendergast, Tony Sherwin, David Keene and Beryl Woodward, S Vaughan.

Photograph credits

Many of the names listed above supplied photographs, plus Margaret Harden, J.A.Forrester postcards; Mr R Smith, Gordon Rex Houle (illustration), National Portrait Gallery; the late Betty Smith, Wendy and family, formerly of 266 Hook Road; Eldred Tims collection; Mark Davison archives; Enid Blyton Dossier by Brian Stewart and Tony Summerfield, Win Nott. Special thanks to Dennis Stickley, John Last, David Tippett-Wilson, Dorchester County Museum and Lilian Swindall, Roy Dack and family, Martin and Ann Draper, Garth and Ingrid Holford, William J Farmer, Pam Neame, Eileen Gould, Christine Wright, Elaine Barron, Gwendolen Freeman's family archives; Fred Thompson, Clive Uridge, Vivien Kitson and Elizabeth Fraser.

Bibliography

Surrey Comet; Kingston Borough News; features by the late Margaret Bellars; The Story of Hook by Marion Bone; A United Family Record by Gwendolen Freeman; Old Royston Volume One by Peter Ketteringham; Royston Crow newspaper; An Oxonian Looks Back by George Chatterton Richards (1947); Oxford Mail; Oxford Journal; Thomas Hardy, A Biography by Michael Millgate; Hardy, by Martin Seymour-Smith; Article by Fran Chalfont, 'Hardy's Residences and Lodgings Part Two' in The Thomas Hardy Journal, February 1993; The Letters of Thomas Hardy collection; Surbiton Past by Richard Statham; old Hook thesis by Gillian Watson; Hook Remembered, Tolworth Remembered, Nightingale Page and Bennett brochures, electoral registers, Ordnance Survey maps, Phillipson's and Kelly's directories and many private documents.

Published by Mark Davison, North Bank, Smoke Lane, Reigate, Surrey, RH2 7HJ. Tel 01737 221215. e-mail: mark.davison1@virgin.net

Printed by Litho Techniques, Godstone Road, Whyteleafe, Surrey.

First edition October 2001

ISBN 0-9534240-5-7

Front cover pictures: Clockwise: Hook Road showing Maythorne Laundry c1951; North Star, Hawthorns and St Quentin plus the 65 bus approaching, c1951; and the old Maypole pre-1904. Back cover: The old White Hart, Hook, in 1889, photographed by John Tims, of Chessington Road, Ewell.

A rare insight into a Victorian bedroom at Hook.

THIS bedroom scene at 3 Laurel Villas, Hook Road, in 1889, was taken by photographer John Tims who travelled the district on a penny farthing. The four villas in this row were pulled down in the mid 1960s to enable a larger playground for St Paul's School to be built. The identity of the woman and her child, at the house four doors down from the North Star, is not recorded by Mr Tims.

By 1923, the four houses were known as Lichfield, Ashleigh, Holmwood and Laverick.

In Lichfield (formerly 1 Laurel Villas) lived Walter and Daisy Whitehead, jewellers at Turners, Surbiton.

The Mutimer family resided at 3 Laurel Villas later in the 1920s but called the house Kuldana. It became 289 Hook Road.

Laurel Villas, Hook Road. No 3 is in the centre.

An advertisement from 1935.

Hook's days of yore

Hook and Southborough used to nestle in the north of the tranquil Surrey countryside. Little changed until late in the 1880s when farmland began to be sold off to developers. The cottagers continued living their humble lives from day to day but in the villas which sprang up as plots of land were sold, families who had made their money from industries in urban towns and cities, moved in for a quiet early retirement. Some of those villas and terraces are still standing, others have long-since vanished. On the following pages there is offered a unique opportunity to re-live those days of yore.

Middleton's laundry was a thriving concern in the 1930s when this aerial photograph was taken. Laundered sheets can be seen in the drying field next to the works. The house at the front of the site, facing the Hook Road, was known as Droitwich and became 121 Hook Road before its demolition and the redevelopment of the site as Verona Drive. In 1924, the occupants of the house were Alice, Edward and William Middleton. The little house approached by way of a path over the meadow was known as Field Cottage and was the home of the Eede family in the 1930s.

Haycroft Farm

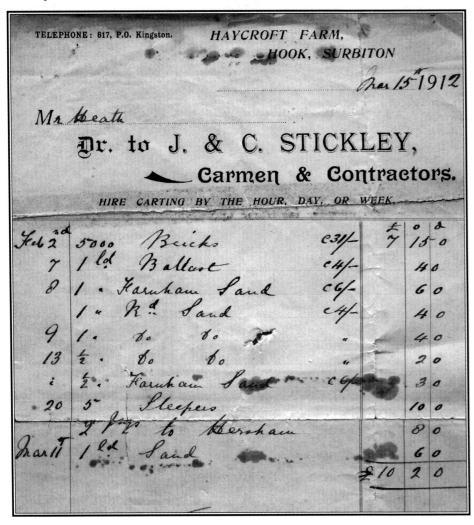

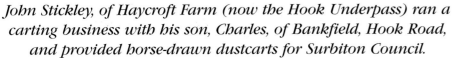

John Stickley, of Haycroft Farm (now the Hook Underpass) ran a carting business with his son, Charles, of Bankfield, Hook Road, and provided horse-drawn dustcarts for Surbiton Council.

A young Hook girl befriends one of the Stickley family's horses at the rear of Bankfield, now 171 Hook Road, in the 1930s. The premises was used by Surbiton Tyres in the 1990s and into the new millennium.

JOHN James Stickley, born in 1832 at Bere Regis, Dorset, arrived in Hook in the mid-Victorian era, having first worked in Kent. He married a London girl, Maria Ann Martin, and they had three children, John, Charles Edward, and Maria Elizabeth. John farmed 20 acres spreading south down from Haycroft Farm towards the site of the Hook Parish Hall. Where the recreation ground was laid out, the Stickleys grew corn. The present-day children's playground was also a wheat field with haybarns at harvest time. Some of the fields used by the Stickleys for farming were bought up by the council in 1901 and used for allotments and the recreation ground. The opening ceremony for the new recreation field was on May 28th 1901. It was named in honour of the new king, Edward VII.

Charles Edward Stickley and his wife, Lily, lived at Bankfield, now 171 Hook Road. The well-known family of Stickleys ran a haulage contractors, much of it horse-drawn, from the yard at the rear of the premises and were contracted out by the local council for many jobs around Surbiton, Tolworth and Hook.

William Edward Stickley learns the ropes at his family's business behind Bankfield, Hook Road, a few yards from today's Ace of Spades roundabout and Hook Underpass.

Stickley family's long link with Hook

STICKLEY is a name which has been closely linked with Hook since the mid Victorian times. There were still a number of Stickleys living in the neighbourhood in the year 2000. One, Dennis, lived in Heath Cottage, Leatherhead Road, Chessington, in retirement and still retained a keen interest in the affairs of Hook. Dennis's brother, Phillip, also remained in the district.

Dennis and Phillip's grandparents were Charles and Lily Stickley, *pictured left*. Their descendants came to Hook from Bere Regis, Dorset, and members of the family farmed many acres of Hook. Other relatives ran the old Southborough Arms, Hook Road, just to the south of Haycroft Road. Some of the family lived at Haycroft Farm, which stood near the Cap in Hand pub of today. Charles Stickley died aged 80 in January 1944, and his wife, in August 1954. They are buried at Hook. The couple had four children, Olive, Edith, Florence and William (*pictured above*). William and his wife, Violet, had a total of nine children, including Dennis Roy, and Phillip.

Hook Road, Southborough, at the beginning of the 1900s. Hook Post Office is on the far left. Behind the hedgerow on the right were two villas, Southborough Hill and Echo Villa and to the rear of these houses, a pond, with bullrushes, which children skated on in winter. Pictured right is Police Constable Charles Nott, the Hook and Southborough bobby on the beat who kept an eye on errant youths.

HOOK'S first post office was at 154 Hook Road, Hook. It is on the extreme left of the picture, at the corner of Gladstone Road. Originally the building was known as Gladstone House. The Butler family ran it during the first part of the 20th century. The pair of semi-detached homes next door were known as 1 and 2 Russell Cottages. The three-storey neighbouring house (now Brook House) was formerly known as Sefton Villas. In modern times, it was converted into flats and the outside painted yellow. Bankfield, then one of the Stickley family's homes, is on the right, together with neighbouring Enfield House. Echo Villa and Southborough Hill are screened by the hedgerow. Harriet Selfe, a bedridden spinster, lived in Southborough Hill in the 1920s and was pestered by menacing boys. Pranksters would also put lighted fireworks through the front door of the dry cleaner's in St Mary's Villas, *left*, but revenge was sweet. The proprietor, Mr Parkinson, appeared on the balcony and threw a bucket of cold water over the lads. On other occasions, boys would nip around the back of Joseph King's off-licence on the corner of Brook Road, steal empties and then apply for a bottle refund at the shop.

Young tearaways would also leap onto the Stickley's hay carts and cause mayhem, or in high spirits, walk past Oakey's grocery shop, shouting: "All Oakey. Keep Pokey!" But the strong arm of the law was never far away. Village bobby, PC Charles Nott, would suddenly appear and try to bring some law and order to the neighbourhood. "Come on lads, go and play on the common."

Anecdotes

Devon Villa, 15 Hook Road:
Home of retired Surbiton chemist Charles Lowe and then his widow, Susannah, from 1878 to about 1908.

Glenholm, 17 Hook Road:
Residence of "quaint and eccentric" grammar school languages master Reginald Nicholls from about 1920 to 1970. He played tennis in the back garden and was a double bassist. While taking part in a light opera at an old people's home in Surbiton, with his violinist sister, and her twin brother, Victor, he collapsed and later died in hospital. The show went on, however. Although the unmarried siblings were Christian Scientists, Reginald is buried in St Paul's, Hook.

Mayfield: 19 Hook Road:
Ernest Gilroy Coward was in residence during the First World War. Next-door neighbours, Sarah, Rosaline and Eglantine Newman, at (Westfield), No 21, spoke of the playwright Noel Coward being a relative and staying there as a child. This seems doubtful and no link has yet been established. Noel Coward lived firstly at Teddington and for a time in Sutton before moving to London as a boy.

The Hollies 25 Hook Road
Ernest Linzell, a printer's artist, lived here at the time of the First World War, and is said to have designed the first £1 Treasury notes, signed by Sir John Bradbury, in August 1914

The farming days were coming to an end for Charles Edward Stickley and for Hook in general in the early 1940s. Charles is seen here in a field next to Middleton's Laundry, now the Verona Drive area, shortly before his death in January 1944 at the age of 80. He had toiled in the fields for most of his life and had known Hook when it was just a rural village covered in meadows and orchards. He is buried in St Paul's churchyard.

as well as 10-shilling and five shilling notes which were never circulated. His daughter, Vivien, was a founder of 1st Hook Guides.

The house's first occupant in 1878 was George Thomas Moore, from Westmoreland, born 1838, a captain with the 42nd Royal Highlanders. He served in Britain and Bengal. He and his Scottish-born wife, Mary, called the villa Tarn Lodge and in 2001 it was still standing as no 25 Hook Road but has long-since been divided into nine flats.

Beechcroft 27 Hook Road: Captain Richard Oakes lived in this five-bedroomed house in the years leading up to the First World War.

Embleton, 39 Hook Road: Before being knocked down, it was the home and surgery of Mr Kenneth Dunn, dentist, in the 1960s.

E. E. BLAKE,
BOOT AND SHOE
Manufacturer,

Alpha Road, Surbiton Hill

Elijah Etwell Blake

ELIJAH Etwell Blake was an extraordinary business entrepreneur in Victorian Hook and Surbiton. Born in Wiltshire in 1835, he later sold boots and shoes from premises at Alpha Road, Surbiton. (Etwell Place was named after him). He then owned the Southborough Brickworks, near Tolworth Road, and is thought to have built and bought several Hook Road houses including Devon Villa in the 1870s. He lived at Vale Cottage, now 75 Hook Road, and was Hook parish overseer.

Harvest time at Hook in Charles Stickley's fields opposite the North Star public house. Note the open-top 65 bus about to return to Ealing. It only went as far as the North Star and then reversed into Orchard Road.

In December 2000, barman John Owens celebrated 30 years working in the North Star at Hook. In 1970, he responded to an agency advertisement while working in St John's Wood and on arrival here, refreshed himself with a pint in the Blackamoor's.

Dennis Stickley with Kit, one of the horses from the family firm at Bankfield, Hook Road, exhibited in a horse show at Hampton Court, when Dennis was about 17 years of age.

J. STICKLEY,
Cowkeeper and Dairyman,
8, ETWELL PLACE,
ALPHA ROAD, SURBITON.

Families Supplied with genuine New Milk at 3d. per Quart.

DOUBLE CREAM at 8d. per Half Pint.

NEW LAID EGGS, &c.

John Stickley sold the Hook farm produce from a shop at Etwell Place, Surbiton Hill.

Dennis Stickley on 13th October 1945 in Signals uniform.

Southborough School

SOUTHBOROUGH Boys' School began life as Tolworth Boys' Central School in Fullers Way North in 1932. The Central School was run as two concerns; one section for the boys, which used the ground floor, and the other for the girls which utilised the first floor. This arrangement continued until the ever-growing population of Hook and Tolworth necessitated the building of a new school.

In the late 1950s, an annex was constructed at the rear of the Ace of Spades petrol station on grazing meadows formerly farmed by the Stickley family.

Mr H.P. Giddy was appointed headmaster of Tolworth Central Boys' School in 1946-7. As the annex evolved into a fully-fledged modern boys' school by September 1962, and was soon renamed Southborough, he transferred to the new site along with all the pupils. The old school became the thriving Tolworth Girls' School.

Southborough School was officially opened in March 1963. Its staff then included R.E. Thomas (woodwork), Rex Darton (maths and careers), P.H. Kerslake (geography) E. 'Stimmy' Stimpson, who retired in the 1960s, W.J. Stephens (woodwork) and Stan Smith (maths, sports and technical drawing).

After Mr Giddy retired in about 1970, his post was filled until December 1986 by John Enstone, who was followed by John Oborn until 1995. He was succeeded by the then deputy head, John Rook, whose mother, Ethel, taught at St Paul's, Hook, for 27 years from 1945.

H.P. Giddy in 1948.

Almost 40 years old: Southborough Boys School, Hook Road, in the summer of 2001.

Southborough Boys' School, built in the late 1950s, replaced this pastoral scene at Hook, as the village's population expanded beyond anyone's imagination. Charles Edward Stickley grazed his horses and cows on this meadow. The view is from the Kingston bypass.

Five-bedroomed house with library

LOT 3.—THE

Freehold Ground Rent

OF

£11 PER ANNUM

Secured upon and arising out of the

DETACHED PRIVATE RESIDENCE

KNOWN AS

" Holmbury,"

HOOK ROAD, UPPER BRIGHTON ROAD,

SURBITON.

Containing Five Bed Rooms, Drawing and Dining Rooms, Library, Kitchen, Scullery, Two W.C.'s and Offices.

Leased for a term of 99 years, from 25th December, 1870, giving a reversion in about 61 years to the estimated rack rental of

£80 PER ANNUM.

Above: details of Holmbury given in a land auction in 1908.

Left: Mrs Hardy's only diary entry from her days in Hook Road.

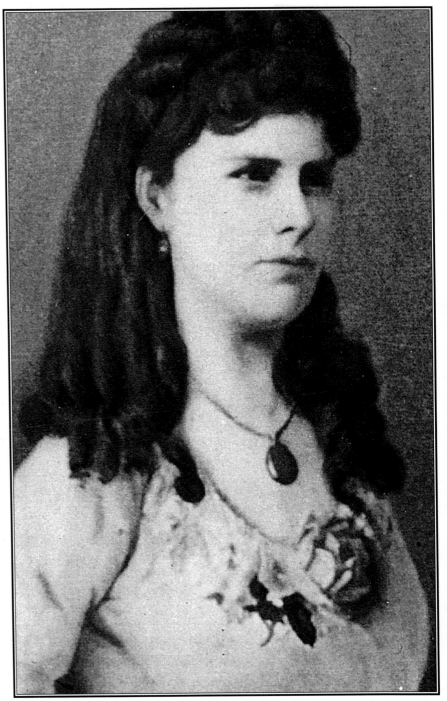

Emma Hardy — five months in the parish of Hook.

St David's Villa, 13 Hook Road, where Hardy lived with his wife, Emma, in 1874-5.

Thomas Hardy in about 1872.

Revealed — Thomas Hardy's home in Hook Road, far from the madding crowd

THOMAS Hardy, the famous author from Dorset, spent the first five months of his married life living in the parish of St Paul's, Hook. And only now, for the first time, has it been established where exactly the house was. The revelation comes after an exhaustive investigation by the author of this book and Colin Prendergast, a modern day resident of Hook, with additional help from others.

The house was St David's Villa which three years later changed its name to Holmbury Cottage and then 13 Hook Road. It was pulled down in 1960 and now Midhurst Court flats occupy the site.

Mr Hardy and his wife, Emma, moved into St David's Villa in the first week of October 1874 after returning from their honeymoon in Paris. Almost immediately, Hardy busied himself making final corrections to the manuscript of the book version of Far From The Madding Crowd which was published the next month and became a runaway success.

The Hardys shared the villa with William David Hughes and his wife, Annie Elizabeth, who moved into the newly-built house in 1873.

The Hughes had a five-year-old daughter, Annie, who Mrs Hardy made a note about in her diary on Tuesday 6th October. The entry said: "St

David's Villa – Surbiton – 5-p.m. Annie & the Retriever playing in the garden with Papa."

Until now, experts on Hardy have claimed that Annie was Mrs Hardy's young cousin and "Papa" was Mrs Hardy's father who, despite his strong disapproval of their marriage, had travelled up from Cornwall to visit the newly-weds. It now seems certain that the "Annie" was Annie Hughes and "Papa" was simply the little girl's aged father, Mr Hughes. The Hardys remained estranged from Emma's father, John Gifford, until his death in 1890. He had regarded Hardy as a "low-born churl".

Hardy's days in Hook

FAR From The Madding Crowd was Thomas Hardy's first major writing achievement. He was living in Hook Road when the tale about rural life in "Wessex" was first published in book form — as a two-part novel — in November 1874.

Hardy and his wife, Emma, were delighted to discover educated ladies reading the book as they arrived in London by train from Surbiton the same month.

Very little is known about the Hardys' Hook days. The author later burnt most of his diaries, letters and memorabilia.

However, it is known that before they left the parish and moved to Westbourne Grove, London, in late March 1875, he started his second major novel, The Hand of Ethelberta. It was a story about a butler's daughter, who successfully poses as a lady, and the four eligible men vying for her attentions. She eventually marries an old landowner called Lord Mountclere and represses her true feelings to enable her to climb up the social ladder.

Hardy may well have sat writing the early chapters of his new novel in the drawing room on the ground floor of St David's, on the side of the house nearest Devon Villa (now 15 Hook Road and rather misleadingly called Hardy House by its restorers in 1994). This side of the house was, in later decades, sub-let to tenants by William and Fanny Cook, the occupiers from the 1930s to the 1950s.

In 1908, St David's — or Holmbury Cottage as it became known — had the freehold up for sale at a London auction along with half a dozen other properties along the Hook Road just north of Vale Road.

It was described as a detached private residence with five bedrooms, drawing and dining rooms, a library, kitchen, scullery, two wcs and offices (rooms for domestic servants). The particulars state that the lease was for 99 years, starting on Christmas Day 1870, which produced from the tenants £80 a year. This compared with £76 for the pair of semis next door, known as Devon Villa and Glenholm (15 and 17 Hook Road).

Back in 1875, St David's was advertised for let, furnished or unfurnished. The advertisement, in the Surrey Comet of Saturday July 17th — about 12 weeks after the Hardys' relocation to London — provides a fascinating insight into what the house was like when the author was in residence.

It says: "Surbiton — to be let immediately, furnished or unfurnished, a substantially built, double fronted detached villa; large dining and drawing rooms, breakfast rooms, large entrance hall and conservatory, four large bed rooms and dressing room; good kitchen, cellar under; scullery and usual domestic offices, two W.C.'s, front and back staircases, large garden, well stocked with flowers, fruit, and ornamental trees and shrubs; large croquet lawn, carriage drive, &c. — For particulars apply to the owner, St. David's-villa, Southboro'-road, Surbiton.

The occupant at the time, Annie Elizabeth Hughes, and her husband, William David Hughes, a retired brewer, aged 67, originally from Oxford, like some other residents of the Hook Road, referred to the road outside their home as "Southborough Road". Then, it was a carriage route between

Hardy's publishers, Smith Elder & Co wrote to him at Hook in March 1875 making him a formal offer of £700 for The Hand of Ethelberta novel.

Surbiton and Leatherhead, surrounded by fields, orchards, and just the occasional group of mid-Victorian cottages, villas, or earlier period mansions such as Brockett (205 Hook Road), Haycroft (now demolished and replaced by houses in Elmcroft Drive) and Orchard Court (opposite today's Cecil Close). There was, of course, no Kingston bypass until the late 1920s.

Thomas Hardy wrote several letters from Hook Road. Some have survived and are in various collections around the world.

The first known letter was written on **9th October 1874** and was sent to his publishers Smith, Elder and Co in London. Addressing his home as St David's Villa, Hook Road, Surbiton SW, he wrote:

Gentlemen,
I have returned to day the copy of my story (Far From The Madding Crowd) *that you were good enough to send for corrections. There are very few, & mainly confined to the opening chapters. A little delay has been caused by my having had to move house since my return from abroad a week ago.*
May I ask to allow my name to appear in the announcements of the book? I enclose a title-page.

Yours very faithfully
Thomas Hardy

Further letters discussing financial arrangements with his publishers followed over the next five months. One sent on **12th November 1874** revealed that Hardy was somewhat baffled over the rights concerning the publication in serial form of Far From The Madding Crowd.

On **17th November 1874**, Hardy wrote from St David's Villa to the prolific novelist and travel writer Katharine Sarah Macquoid to thank her for her letter and give his views on the roles of women in literature.

He said: "The question whether women of ordinary types should or should not be depicted as the heroines of novels is such a nice one that it is difficult to discuss it in writing. I myself, I must confess, have no great liking for the perfect woman of fiction, but this may be for purely artistic reasons."

The author seemed to enjoy the debate with her and visited Macquoid's home a few days later.

On **24th November 1874** and **3rd January 1875**, Hardy wrote to publisher William Tinsley seeking a release of the copyright of his 1871 pastoral comedy novel, Under The Greenwood Tree. Hardy had given it to Tinsley for £30 but was invited to fork out the princely sum of £300 to get it back. Hardy had unsuccessfully tried to meet Tinsley in November at the publisher's London office.

In a letter to New York publisher Henry Holt on **11th February 1875**, Hardy asked for a specimen copy of the America edition of Far From The Madding Crowd for his perusal, adding that in England, the book had "met with a success which had exceeded our expectations."

The icy weather of the early spring of 1875 also lent itself to comment. The "abominable east winds" whistled around St David's Villa and Hardy attributed his relatives' poor health to the inclement conditions in a letter written on **5th March 1875**.

Following a letter to publishers Smith, Elder & Co on **27th February 1875**, requesting definite terms for allowing them to publish his new novel, The Hand of Ethelberta, Hardy and Emma made a decision to move nearer to the centre of London. Everything was happening in Hardy's literary world and he wanted to be where the action was.

He wrote to publisher George Smith to say he would be "coming to Town for three months on account of Ethelberta" and on **19th March 1875** prepared to leave his home in Hook Road to move to rented rooms in Paddington. The new novel would also feature some London scenes and he wanted to capture these accurately in his writings.

Writing to house agents Townly and Boniwell, *(at Claremont Road, junction with the foot of St Mark's Hill, Surbiton)*, Hardy asked the firm to warehouse four boxes of the couple's belongings, probably because their new lodgings at Paddington were furnished.

Two of the boxes contained books, and another, books and linen. The remaining box was filled with "sundries". It is written elsewhere that these boxes held the Hardys' "entire worldly goods."

So why did the Hardys choose Surbiton for their first marital home?

It is likely that a friend of the author's gave them a helping hand to find the accommodation. Trading in Surbiton Park Terrace, a few hundred yards from where the Assembly Rooms were built, was Francis Honeywell, who, like Hardy, hailed from Dorset and was the same age as Thomas and apparently a friend of old.

Mr Honeywell had come to Surbiton as a young man and had set up a music shop in the terrace which had grown from strength to strength. By the late Victorian period his shop contained more than 100 pianos.

A century later, Elsie Honeywell, a grand-daughter of Francis Honeywell, called at Hardy's well-known Dorset home, Max Gate, and in a conversation, told the owners that Francis was a friend of the author.

Honeywell was well respected in Surbiton and a familiar figure in town. He probably put in a good word at the offices of Townly and Boniwell, asking them to let him know if some rooms became available for letting to his Dorsetshire pal and his new wife. The rooms to let at St David's had not

Townly and Boniwell estate agents, Surbiton — used by Thomas Hardy in March 1875.

apparently been advertised in the press.

There is no other likely explanation why a couple coming afresh to London after a foreign honeymoon would stumble over what was then such an out-of-the-way place as Hook Road, which still had the Southborough tollgate operating 100 yards away, preventing vehicular access to the Hook *(Southborough)* Road without payment of a halfpenny, except by those living in the immediate locality.

Francis Honeywell's music shop in Surbiton Park Terrace more than a century ago. Mr Honeywell was a friend of Thomas Hardy. Honeywell and Hardy were born in Dorset at almost the same time — in 1839 and 1840 and Francis was brought up in St Thomas Street, Weymouth. This is just yards from where, in 1869, Hardy worked for a spell as an architect in the offices of Mr G.R.Crickmay. The Honeywell family traded as chairmakers, outfitters and tailors. Francis's parents, John and Mary ran the store and employed five staff. Hardy lodged at Wooperton Street where there is a plaque above the front door in the small terrace.

In search of Hardy's home

THE long hunt for Hardy's home in Hook Road has ended but how was the mystery solved? Mark Davison and fellow researcher Colin Prendergast, of Somerset Avenue, Hook, spent two years of their free time delving into boxes of dusty old documents, chasing clues and probing the history of old Hook houses.

Their quest took them all over the country, by phone and in person. The puzzle led to Penzance. Then they hurried to Hastings, rushed to Royston and were then orientated to Oxford. But they were plagued by red herrings along the way — in Dublin, Deptford and Dorset.

All that was known of Hardy's home was that it was called St David's Villa and it was in Hook Road. No street directories of the 1870s carried Hardy's name. And only one directory listed St David's Villa — the Kelly's for Kingston in 1874. Where in Hook Road it did not say. The occupant's name was given as William David Hughes. There were no further clues.

Who was William David Hughes? The census of both 1871 and 1881 failed to list a St David's Villa. But it was probably not built in 1871. The only Hughes in Hook Road in 1881 were two unmarried sisters, Mary and Anna. They lived in one of the pair of semi-detached villas which became known as Mayfield and Westfield. These villas stood until about 1989 between Thornhill Road and Maypole Motors and became 19 and 21 Hook Road.

In 1881, Anna was 30 years old and Mary, 33. Anna was born in Westminster and Mary in the Strand. Their mother, Ellen Eliza Agutter, resided at the three-storey house with her second husband, William Agutter, a retired mercantile who founded Deptford Ragged School. Were these Hughes girls related to the William David Hughes living at St David's Villa? And, if so, was St David's the earlier name of Westfield and Mayfield? If the girls were related, it would be a certainty that this was where Thomas Hardy rented his rooms in 1874-5.

Colin, who works at the Family Records Centre, in London, sacrificed many lunch hours trying to prove the link.

Earlier hopes were raised when he learnt that the Hughes' girls' late father was named William Hughes. It seemed that the mystery was nearly over. Was he the William David Hughes? If so, he was Hardy's landlord or flatmate.

The joy of the discovery was dulled, however, when it was discovered from earlier London census returns that William Hughes had died in the 1850s. He couldn't be the one after all. So did he have a son, William David Hughes? Tedious trawls were made through the records, turning the house detectives' attention to Bournemouth, Brighton, Belfast and beyond. With the help of a professional family tree researcher, John Finch, and an Irish investigator, it was finally established that there was no evidence anywhere of a William David Hughes linked to the Hughes family at Westfield and Mayfield. Everyone was downcrested. All this effort had seemingly been in vain.

> Southborough, Hook road,
> continuation of Brighton road.
> Wickam Miss, 1
> Edgar Edward, esq. 2 } Southborough
> Laxton Charles, esq. 3 } terrace
> Henfrey Mrs. 4
> Castledine Wm. farmer (Brook farm)
> Eves Francis, market gardener
> Wood Wm. Randall, brick maker
> Hurren James, florist
> Shutte Lancelot Blagdon, esq. (Elm cottage)
> Wilson Lindsay, esq. (Lindsay lodge)
> Clayton Mrs. (Haycroft)
> Clode William, esq. (Brockett house)
> Monk Nathaniel, esq. (Pelham house)

Hook Road, Southborough in 1867 - seven years before Thomas Hardy arrived.

How could the investigation proceed? There was apparently nothing more to go on.

John Finch, using a computerised search of the 1881 census found there were at least 5,700 other males called William Hughes alive at the time. It was an impossible task to check them. There were far fewer William D Hughes entries, however. Each one was laboriously vetted and remarkably, only four turned out to have the middle name David. One was a rigger in the north west; another an unemployed chef in Somerset and yet another was only a child. Further inquiries on all of them drew a blank.

Daunted, and with dwindling enthusiasm, Colin re-examined the deaths of all males called William David Hughes over a 50-year period. One who initially aroused interest was a man by this name who died in Hastings in the bitterly cold December of 1890.

Mark Davison drove to Hastings and located his grave on a windy hilltop cemetery. There were barely any words on the tombstone. His death certificate was applied for. It gave his Hastings address as 19 Park Road. Street directories listed him as living earlier in Bohemia Road, St Leonards. Who was he? The cemetery office looked up the grave records and said he was a retired brewer.

Further details of this 'suspect' were found on a Hastings census record for 1881. He was born in Oxford and his wife was Annie Elizabeth Hughes. They had a child when she was 45 years old and he 56. The child took her mother's name, Annie Elizabeth Hughes. The grave was photographed and added to the 'wanted' file.

The grave of former Hook Road resident, William David Hughes, who shared a house with Hardy.

Colin had meanwhile established that a William David Hughes, a brewer, had married at Royston, Herts, in 1867 and this turned out to be the same man. He was a prime suspect for having lived at St David's Villa, Hook, but there was no evidence whatsoever.

By now, all the 'suspects' were being 'killed off' one by one – the only survivor was "Hastings man" Hughes. In February 2001, all the stops were pulled out. Every move of Hastings Man was put under scrutiny.

Colin visited libraries across London, looking for his past addresses and then checking them against census returns for those locations. Hughes was found living in the rural village of Bassingbourn, near Royston, with his wife and two-year-old daughter in 1871.

Mark and Colin then flicked through the pages of the Hastings directories and found that Hughes first moved to the seaside town in 1876. When did he leave Royston? This was a vital question. Was he at Hook in the intervening years?

On a cold and sunny Saturday morning, Mark set off for Cambridge and sat in the central library looking at the few only surviving electoral registers for Royston. By a stroke of luck, they covered the 1870s. What he found out within a few minutes was so exciting he bought the surprised staff a box of chocolates. William David Hughes changed his address in 1873 to . . . "St David's Villa, Southborough Road, Surbiton Surrey" but could still vote in Royston because he was still letting a house there. The seemingly unsolvable mystery was soon to be unravelled.

How mystery was solved

THE biggest clue in identifying Thomas Hardy's Hook Road home was to be the name of the fellow occupant, or perhaps landlord, William David Hughes. And after two years of tiresome searching for the Mr Hughes in question, the right man was eventually picked out. It enabled further vital evidence to be put on the table which would eventually pinpoint the location of the house.

Retired brewer Hughes was born in Oxford in about 1808, the son of James Hughes, also a brewer. He was 59 and a bachelor when he married widow Annie Elizabeth Matthews in the pretty Cambridgeshire village of Meldreth, near Royston, in 1867.

His 44-year-old bride was widowed the year before and ran the chemists and druggists in Royston High Street, which she took over from her late husband, Joseph, after his death.

The shop was extremely popular in town. Joseph's funeral had been a major event in Royston. After all, the shop had been in the Matthews' family since 1802.

Annie had a son, Ernest, by her marriage to the chemist. She also had a daughter, Augusta, who married an Arthur Taylor, a renowned chemist for many years in Hastings.

Ernest died in 1902 after a cut to his finger led to blood poisoning. The business continued in the hands of Ernest's wife, Rosa, and son, also Ernest. But when Rosa died, the son let it go to rack and ruin.

Son, Ernest, became an intelligent recluse. He failed to stock up the shop and it fell into disuse. Even though customers boycotted it, Ernest went through the motions and opened the doors each day. It is said he did not wash and wore the same clothes for 30 years. His toe nails were so long, they formed a type of cap around his toes. His boots were so worn, there were no soles and his bare feet were in contact with the ground. His old raincoat was tied up with a belt and his long hair stuck through holes in his hat. In 1943, he was found dead after being struck by a branch while picking apples in his orchards. He had lain on the ground undiscovered for two days.

He was known as Barmy Matthews. Only about four people turned up to his funeral, unlike his father's where the town had virtually shut down for the day and a great ceremony had taken place.

Barmy Matthews was 58 when he died and he was the last of that famous Royston family. He left several properties and land in his estate. Woolworths is now on the site of the Matthews' chemist's.

Back in Victorian times, the shop also had a wine and spirits department and it is here that Barmy's grandmother, Annie, may have met her future husband, the former brewer William David Hughes.

What took them to Hook in 1873 is unclear. Perhaps it was a wish to get away from the family and gossip over her speedy remarriage and the birth of baby Annie at the not-so-young age of 45.

Whatever the reason, they left Royston and set up home at St David's Villa, on the opposite side of Hook Road to the old Maypole

'Barmy' Matthews and what is probably his ageing mother Rosa, outside their chemist's shop in Royston, Herts. Barmy's grandmother left the shop to live at St David's Villa, Hook. Inset: Barmy's father, Ernest.

pub and a few hundred yards up from the junction with Ditton Road and what was then the Southborough Gate tollpoint.

Their little daughter, Annie, was four years old when they arrived in 1873 and aged five when Thomas Hardy and his wife, Emma, moved into what was probably the right hand side of the same five-bedroomed villa in the autumn of the following year.

Mrs Hardy's diary entry for 6th October 1874 noted that Annie was playing in the garden with the Retriever and Papa at 5pm on that day. It is recorded in other archives that the same day dawned cold and almost frosty but clouded over as gales lashed the south east in the late afternoon and evening. Annie was probably quite excited by the trees swishing in the high winds as Emma Hardy observed her little companion playing outside with the child's 66-year-old father, "Papa".

The Hardys endured one of the coldest Decembers in three decades while at Hook. And as the snow fell on one day, Hardy looked out of the window of St David's at the feathery flakes and wrote a poem, Light Snowfall After A Frost.

The young Annie and her parents left St David's, Hook Road, in 1875-6 and moved to Hastings where Mrs Hughes' seven grandchildren lived. Obviously, she was missing seeing them regularly and wanted to be closer at hand.

When Mr Hughes died in 1890, his wife and Annie, now 22, stayed only one more year at the seaside town before moving back to Royston.

Within a year, young Annie had married a classical professor, George Chatterton Richards, who became a top Oxford master and vicar of the University Church. And it was he who was found to own St David's Villa in a 1914 rates survey. The house was on the site of 13 Hook Road, and had been renamed Holmbury as long ago as 1876.

Barmy Matthews. A caricature by Wink.

Thomas Hardy's first marital home, St David's Villa, Hook Road, was probably owned by the forefathers of Reverend George Chatterton Richards, (above) a professor of Greek at Oriel College, Oxford. He married Annie Elizabeth Hughes, daughter of William David Hughes, in 1891. The former vicar of St Mary the Virgin university church, Oxford, is listed as the villa's owner in 1914. This 1926 picture, by Lafayette, is from the National Portrait Gallery, London.

Clergyman associated with Hardy's home

Owner of St David's Villa

THIS was the man who owned the house in Hook Road where Thomas Hardy lived for almost six months. He is Reverend George Chatterton Richards, who was one of the country's most prominent professors of Greek.

He was the son-in-law of William David Hughes, the man who lived at the author's home in Hook Road, but of whom nothing was known by Hardy researchers until now.

The vicar was married to Annie Elizabeth Hughes, nee Matthews, who as a small child, was seen by Mrs Hardy playing in the garden with the retriever dog.

Before the First World War, prime minister Lloyd George conducted a mammoth and controversial survey of all properties in the country to list their rateable values. The list survives in the public records office at Kew but is in a grubby condition.

The blackened document reveals that the house, Holmbury Cottage, was owned by Rev Richards of 13 Canterbury Road, Oxford. This is the address that the professor was living at when tutoring at Oriel College.

What has not yet been established is whether the clergyman's direct descendants or his in-laws, the Hughes or Matthews, had St David's Villa in Hardy's time — 1874-5.

Rev Richards was born in Churchover, Warwickshire, in 1867. His father, John, was a corn miller in Rugby employing one man. Another son also intended to go into the ministry but died in Cardiff in the 1890s.

Young Richards did not have a happy childhood. He later wrote: "Of my early years I remember hardly anything but ill health and misery."

At the age of seven, he managed to get into Rugby School, close to his home. A small change in admission rules meant he was lucky.

"So it came about that an ignorant urchin entered the school in which he was to remain for 10 years," he reminisced in old age. "As I rose in school my position became more tolerable."

He became a star pupil, befriended by the staff and even mingled in their social circles. While breakfasting at the Master's house one day, "there entered, with the manner of a sleek and over-fed cat, one man I recognised as Matthew Arnold."

At the Rugby home of a tutor, Linnaeus Cumming, he met his future wife, Annie. Why teenager Annie was there is not clear, but the Cumming family were close friends of the Hughes. It was by then more than a decade since she had been living in Hook. She had since then lived in Hastings and then at Meldreth, near Royston.

By 1891, the "star pupil" had graduated at Balliol College, Oxford, where he obtained first classes in classical moderations and in Greats, besides winning the Ireland and Craven Scholarship and the Derby Scholarship.

The brainy "BA" boy had been appointed Fellow of Hertford College, Oxford, but in 1891 became professor of Greek at the University College, Cardiff, where he remained until 1897.

He then was offered the post of tutor at Oriel College, Oxford, and in 1898, he was also made chaplain.

Meanwhile, he had got married to Annie. The wedding, in 1891, was at Meldreth Church, near Royston.

Both the bride and the groom's fathers by now were dead. The chemist, Ernest Matthews, was among those present at the service.

The early married years of the couple in South Wales were described as very happy. Mr Richards said his only regret was that he did not learn the Welsh language. He was ordained a deacon and priest at Llandoff, Cardiff.

In 1899, he went to Athens for a year to take part in a major archaeological dig.

In 1923 he became vicar of St Mary the Virgin Church, Oxford — the "University Church". It is today the most visited parish church in the country. He held the post until 1927 when he moved to Durham where he became professor of Greek and classical literature in Durham university. In 1934, he resigned on grounds of poor health and returned to Oxford, where his last years were spent. He had remained a Fellow of Oriel until 1932.

The Richards's had several children. His daughter, Olive, moved to South Africa and lost a son in the last war in Italy. Daughter Silvia married Rev William Henry Draper and a son, Martin, was still alive in the year 2001, living in Northumberland aged 78.

Rev Richards died in 1951; Annie in 1953. They are buried in Wolvercote Cemetery, Oxford, and in a grave close to that of author J.R.R. Tolkien, author of Lord of The Rings and The Hobbit.

It appears that the "wealthy" side of the family was that of the vicar's wife. She left £9,000 in her will. A tidy sum in 1953.

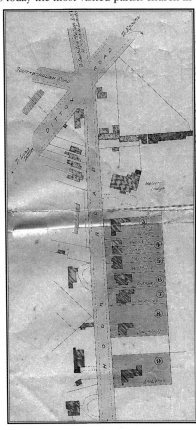

The northern end of Hook Road in 1908 showing Holmbury (St David's Villa).

Author was 'great friends' with musician

Surbiton link with Hardy

SURBITON seemed an unlikely place for Thomas Hardy and his wife to come and live for nearly six months after their wedding in 1874. How did he end up staying in rooms at the unlikely address of Hook Road?

The answer almost certainly lies with the author's friendship with Francis Honeywell who was a noted musician from Weymouth, Dorset, who moved to Kingston in 1860.

Honeywell, who was born in Weymouth in November 1839, came to live in Surbiton Park Terrace. He was an expert on the piano, organ, violin, and cello and he composed music, including a piece called The Surbiton Galop and the Hampton Court Quadrille. At the age of 21 he was organist of St Mary Woolnoth, Weymouth. In 1877 he became organist of All Saints, Kingston, and performed this duty for 20 years.

Francis Honeywell.

He was a man with a quiet sense of humour and a love of practical jokes. This sometimes involved the use of electricity for he was absolutely fascinated with this new source of power. His was the first shop in the Kingston area to have electricity.

Honeywell's premises were visited by Surbiton and Kingston folk who were seeking to buy pianofortes or who wanted music lessons from this artistic genius.

The teaching side of the business was later transferred to The Elms, Surbiton Road.

Honeywell was also a keen cyclist and in 1874 he launched the annual Hampton Court cycle meet. It remained a major national event for many years. In 1872, he won the medal for the Amateur Championship of England.

Honeywell had seven children. Some were born in Surbiton, others in Weymouth and he was married twice.

His son, William Mozart Honeywell, took over the business when Francis

Hardy's friend, Francis "Frank" Honeywell, the musician from Weymouth who moved to Surbiton Park Terrace and started up a successful music shop. Honeywell was organist at All Saints Church, Kingston, from 1877-1897.

died in 1903. There had apparently been a fall-out with one of his sons, John Sebastian Honeywell.

John married and a resulting child, also John, still had offspring alive in 2001. One of them was Sheila Veryard (nee Honeywell), of Tonbridge. She recalled her aunt Beatrice, one of the Surbiton musician's daughters often relating how Hardy and her father were "great friends". Hardy, too, was a keen violinist.

Francis Honeywell's great grand-daughter, Sheila Veryard (nee Honeywell), pictured in the year 2001 at her home in Tonbridge where she taught violin and viola. Sheila related how her great grandfather and Hardy were friends.

Mrs Veryard, born in 1929, a year after Hardy's death, said: "Aunt Beat used to say how the Hardys sometimes came to Kingston to visit her father. We did not take much notice. I only wish we had listened more. Aunt Beat knew Tom well enough to call him Tom. He wasn't 'Mr Hardy'."

Francis Honeywell's other great grand-daughter, Ann, verified the tale as did Ann and Sheila's mother, Elsie, aged 96 in 2001.

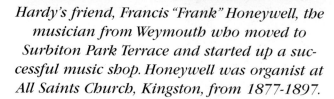

Beatrice Honeywell.

Annie Elizabeth Richards, the daughter of William David Hughes, who lived with her parents as a child at St David's Villa, Hook Road, at the same time as Thomas Hardy in 1874-5, is seen sitting on the wall at a family get-together at Oxford in 1950. She was by then 81 years old.

Emma Hardy wrote in her 1874 diary about young Annie playing in the garden of St David's with a retriever.

Annie was always a keen dog-lover and in the photo is her overfed terrier, Pete.

Standing at the back is Annie's grandson, Martin Draper. Holding the dog is Annie's daughter, Mary, prevented from marrying by her "powerful" mother. Sitting on the step is Martin Draper's wife, Ann. She is holding their first baby, Stephen — Annie's great grandson, then aged five months. In the year 2001 Stephen was a senior lecturer in psychology at Glasgow University.

A rough copy of a letter Hardy sent to a publisher while at Hook.

A family garden party at Holmbury, 13 Hook Road, at Whitsun 1938, hosted by Hook builder, decorator William Henry Cook, (standing), who moved to the house four years earlier. From left to right are William's relations: Fanny Cook, his wife; Roy Dack, grandson; Florence Dack, his daughter; Clarence Dack, son-in-law; Minnie (standing) his eldest daughter; Albert Henry Cook, his son; Raymond Cook, his grandson; Graham Cook, another grandson; Win, his daughter-in-law; Selina Cook, his daughter; and the head of grandson Peter Dack. It was in this garden that Thomas Hardy's wife, Emma, watched little Annie Hughes playing with a retriever on 6th October 1874.

William and Fanny Cook. William was for many years a builder, decorator and undertaker trading from 73-75 Hook Road, between Vale Road North and and Vale Road South. He retired in 1934 and moved to Holmbury, 13 Hook Road, where he lived until his death in 1958. They are pictured in Holmbury's garden in retirement. Mrs Cook died in 1952. Midhurst Court was built on the site. The houses in the background form Malvern Close, off Malvern Road.

William Henry Cook leaning on the gate of his home at Vale Cottage, now 75 Hook Road, next to the carpenter's workshop and office of his business. The bungalow office was later pulled down. Behind the office was a builder's yard and wood store and an exit to Vale Road North. William's son, Frederick, can be seen in the background. No 75 became de Carle hairdresser's.

W.H. Cook, builder, 73-75 Hook Road

THE Cook family were associated throughout the 20th century with their building and decorating trade based in Hook Road between Vale Road North and Vale Road South.

Founder William Henry Cook, moved to the area after marrying Fanny Ellingworth at Oakham, Rutland, in 1893. It is believed he first arrived in the Hook and Tolworth area when he came to work as a carpenter for a builder based in or near the Maypole garage yard, next to Malvern Lodge. After moving several times within the local area, William and Fanny settled firstly at 119 Cotterill Road, Tolworth, where he started his building firm. By 1911, he had transferred the business to 69-71 (now 73-75) Hook Road. The firm also traded as an undertaker at this time. By October 1923, the business had a telephone installed — Kingston 1785. On William's retirement in 1934, his son Albert Henry Cook took over the firm and continued to trade for many years.

Croquet lawn, redcurrant bushes, a kitchen garden and pots of jam

Memories of Holmbury, 13 Hook Road

VIVID memories of Holmbury, 13 Hook Road, have been recalled by two of William Henry Cook's grandsons. Roy Dack and Bob Cook both remember visiting their grandfather as children and playing in the large rooms and in the spacious garden which had fruit trees and many redcurrant and blackcurrant bushes.

Bob said his aunts sometimes played croquet on the lawn.

Roy, born in 1932, who became a grandfather himself and lived in retirement at Elm Road, Hook, said Holmbury was a double-fronted, two-storey house with a little front garden with laurel and laburnham trees. Neighbouring houses had holly growing at the front.

"In its original state there was probably a gravel driveway. One of my uncles used to drive his cars up to the front of the house. The quite large front door was in the middle and it had a single step up to it. As you went in you then had to go through another door into the hall. There was a room on the left and a room on the right and a conservatory on the right hand side of the house and a door on the side into the conservatory. There was another glass door inside with frost-patterned glass and stained windows which took you up from there to the left and the left again. There were big spacious rooms. After the first little landing, you turned left and there were a few steps which went into an extension which came down from the side of the house. My grandfather used to sub let those rooms.

"There was a big garden and we used to have tea on the lawn in the 1930s," said Roy, who before moving to Elm Road had also lived in Priory Road.

Roy said that in the garden were apple, pear and plum trees and many raspberry bushes. A vegetable plot was at the side.

"Grandpa kept chickens at the bottom of the garden. I think that he supplied most of the vegetables he grew. My mum commented that she used to pay grandpa for the vegetables and then granny gave her the money back."

He said there was a cellar in the house but as children, they were not allowed to venture down into it.

He said a second staircase at the back of the house was not used in his grandfather's time. It led from a room they used as a pantry. "There was a small floored staircase which went up to the servants' quarters but it was piled up with jars of home-made jam. There were old servants' bells in the house. They were in the right-hand-side room.

There was a handle for the bells in the front room, used only on Sundays and on special occasions when in winter, open fires were lit.

"My grandfather, we understand, made the pews in the choir stalls at St Paul's Church and he pumped the organ and was known as an assistant organist."

William and Fanny moved into Holmbury in 1934, when William retired, but there is some question mark over whether they rented the house or bought it.

Since its earliest days — when it was known as St David's Villa — right up to the late 1920s and perhaps for a much longer time, the original occupants, the Hughes and Richards family seemed to have had an interest in the property.

After the Thomas Hardy's occupancy, William and Annie Hughes and their daughter, Annie, moved to Hastings in the latter half of 1875 or early the following year. But members of the family were to return in the mid 1920s. In 1875, Mr and Mrs E. Whistler then moved in, although it seems Mrs Mary Whistler, then 50, was soon to be widowed at the age of 50.

Arthur Paxon was in residency by 1884 and his place was taken by law publisher's clerk, Herbert Maxwell, and his Surbiton-born wife, Amy, and their two children by 1891. The Maxwells left in 1902 and Arthur Frederick Sells took over. He stayed until 1908 when Charles Brook moved in.

Rev George Chatterton Richards, husband of Annie who lived at the house as a child in the 1870s, is listed as the owner in about 1914 although, oddly, only as the owner of the plot of land adjoining in 1912-13 and 1915.

The occupants around the time of the Great War were Percival and Margaret Hall. By 1923, only Margaret is registered at the house and it seems to have been unoccupied in 1924.

The following year, Rev and Mrs Richards' son, Richard and his wife, Olive, are in residence, probably with their sons, Peter and John. They had moved to South Africa by 1927 where they were visited by Rev Richards. It is possible that Annie Richards did not go on the voyage to see her family, for she is listed as being briefly back at Holmbury in 1927, sharing the home with Samuel Ernest Cook, son of William Henry Cook, and Samuel's wife.

Mr and Mrs Samuel Cook remained at the house for three years after which a long list of lodgers were living there until 1934 when William Henry Cook and his wife, Fanny, were in residence until their deaths in the 1950s.

William Henry Cook and his wife Fanny pictured in the garden of Holmbury, 13 Hook Road, in 1943 on what may have been the occasion of their golden wedding.

Hardy's Hook Road poem

A Light Snow-Fall after Frost

ON the flat road a man at last appears:
How much his whitening hairs
Owe to the settling snow's mute anchorage,
And how much to a life's rough pilgrimage,
One cannot certify.

The frost is on the wane,
And cobwebs hanging close outside the pane
Pose as festoons of thick white worsted there,
Of their pale presence no eye being aware
Till the rime made them plain.

A second man comes by;
His ruddy beard brings fire to the pallid scene:
His coat is faded green;
Hence seems it that his mien
Wears something of the dye
Of the berried holm-trees that he passes nigh.

The snow-feathers so gently swoop that though
But half an hour ago
The road was brown, and now is starkly white,
A watcher would have failed defining quite
When it transformed it so.

Hidden by holly — the Maypole Guest House, 18 Hook Road, could hardly be seen from the street until July 2001 when the holly was replaced with a wooden fence. The house was built in 1902 but the hedgerow pre-dated the building. The guest house is opposite Midhurst Court, the site of Holmbury Cottage. Holm and holly are similar in appearance.

Lych Gate and Church   Long Ditton

Hardy visited St Mary's Church, Long Ditton, on 19th December 1874 and wrote that the snow on the graves was a "perfect piece of cynicism in Nature".

A sprig of holly picked from the rambling bushes outside the Maypole Guest House, Hook Road, in June 2001. The ancient hedgerow, partly cut down the following month and replaced by a timber fence, is directly opposite the villa where Hardy lived. He probably wrote this poem while sitting in the front room of 13 Hook Road in the bitter December of 1874, looking out at the snow falling onto Hook Road. The manuscript says under the poem: "Near Surbiton". Another poem, Snow in the Suburbs, dates from the period. The remaining hedgerow still stands outside No 20, once the surgery of Dr Mowll, and must be preserved. Nos 18 and 20 were formerly called Derrynane and Beresford.

Between Vale Roads North and South there has been a row of cottages since the 1870s or earlier, housing a variety of businesses and small shops. The name board of A.H.Cook, builder, can be seen displayed at Vale Cottage, then 71 Hook Road, now Michael de Carle hairdressers, 75 Hook Road. An ironmonger's on the right sold household items such as the galvanised iron bathtubs seen propped up against the wall of what was then 73 Hook Road (later No 77), from 1936 to beyond the millennium, the home of Ron Hook (inset). In the year 2001, 'Mr Hook of Hook' was a nonagenarian. Ashby's, grocer's, traded for many years in the terrace.

Staff of Homeware in the 1930s. The building — now the site of Budgens supermarket — was formerly Moon's fruit stores. The factory staff made mops, polishes and other kitchenware from the 1930s until the mid 1960s. It was run by Mr Axton and Messrs Long.

Five shilling flights from Hook Aerodrome

In the early 1930s, farmer Broom's fields behind Kelvin Grove were used as an aerodrome for short pleasure flights on Sundays costing five shillings. Some young boys remember being allowed to travel together for half a crown each. One pilot died when his parachute failed to open as he plunged from a stricken aircraft into the fields alongside Woodstock Lane South.

Tragic end in blaze for spinster sisters

THE founder of a ragged school in a desperately poor part of London came to retire in Hook with his wife and two step-daughters in 1878. William Agutter took pity on the underfed boys and girls who lived in squalid and overcrowded terraces in Deptford. Sometimes up to 20 people would share a house and it wasn't uncommon for the malnourished youngsters to die. Those who came to this Congregationalist's newly-formed school in 1844 often arrived barefoot.

Their behaviour was sometimes quite wild and on one occasion, Mr Agutter had stones thrown at his head which resulted in bleeding.

The commercial clerk had a mental breakdown in 1864 and in despair, he handed back to the school a Bible which volunteers had presented to him. Thankfully, he recovered and in 1867, the Bible was "gladly received" back into his possession.

In 1879, at the age of 72 and weary from his long spell in dirty Deptford, he rented a new semi-detached house at Hook, which he called Hook Villa. It later became known as Mayfield and from the late 1940s for 30 years was home to Ronald and Nora Ireland and their family, now in retirement in Penzance, Cornwall.

Mr Agutter spent five years at Hook Villa (later 19 Hook Road). He lived there with his second wife, Ellen, the widow of William John Hughes, a civil engineer from Dublin, and Ellen's two unmarried daughters, Mary, a teacher, and Annie.

In 1885, the family moved to Brighton but the same year, Mr Agutter died from cancer on a visit to Croydon. Newly widowed, Mrs Agutter remained in Brighton with her daughters and they started up a business as proprietors of a patent medicine.

Little is known about the concoction they invented, but the family continued trading for more than 20 years. The spinsters, together with an unmarried older sister, Ellen, remained in Brighton after their mother died in 1894, aged 74.

Then tragedy struck. On 13th December 1920, Ellen, then 75, and Mary, 73, perished in a blaze at their home, 116 Springfield Road, Preston. Ellen's severely charred body had fallen through a ceiling, so bad were the flames. An inquest decided both died from suffocation after the fire, which accidentally started when spilled paraffin from an upturned stove in a first floor bedroom ignited.

Annie died the next year in a mental hospital at Wivelsfield, Sussex.

Sad demise: Hook Villa (Mayfield) and Westfield, 19&21 Hook Road, being demolished in 1989. Yew Tree House House stands on the site.

Southernhay, 207 Hook Road, in May 1938 when the Holford family were in residence. Enid Blyton had lived here, 1920-4.

Southernhay after Enid Blyton

THIS was the house in Hook Road where Enid Blyton lived from 1920-4 when she was a governess for the Thompson family.

During her years in Hook, the old Victorian house, Southernhay — 207 Hook Road — was covered with creeper and had extensive grounds and tennis courts. In the 1930s, the Holford family moved in. They previously lived in Uxbridge Road, Kingston. Mr Sidney Holford was a top Harley Street dentist.

The family lived at Southernhay until the Second World War when they moved to Upper Brighton Road, Surbiton. One of their children was called Garth and as an octogenarian, he looked back with affection on his happy childhood times at the house.

There was a moment of hilarity in his youth when the youngsters were playing golf in the garden.

Garth took a swing with his father's golf club and to his horror, the stick shot out of his hand and flew into the next door garden of the prominent local resident Walter Willcocks, JP.

"There was wire netting around our garden to stop the balls going over but it went over the top and over the conservatory wall and into the Willcocks' conservatory. I went round to retrieve the golf club and to apologise for what happened.

"Mr Willcocks said 'Don't worry, I already know.' After the church service at St Paul's, the Willcocks's came round for a drink before lunch. Mr Willcocks turned round to my younger brother as he gave me two shillings and sixpence 'for being so honest and dashing round to tell me'.

"My brother, who was only given two shillings, was quite put out and said to me 'I think I'll hit a golf ball in there!'"

The Willcocks family allowed the Holford children to play in their garden which stretched down to Fuller's Way. Their house was called Brockett and is 205 Hook Road. It is still standing today, along with Southernhay.

Garth befriended an elderly lady, Mrs Bradford, who lived in a bungalow in Fullers Way. She died just three months before her 100th birthday and Garth was amazed to learn that she had left him some money in her will as the main beneficiary. On one visit he was aghast to find her standing precariously on a table trying to change a bulb. He believes she liked him because his father was a dentist and her son had been a dentist prior to the Great War.

The back view of Southernhay seen from the tennis courts when the Holfords lived there in the 1930s. In the centre, upstairs, was Sidney Holford's dressing room and on the right, Sidney and Florence's bedroom. Downstairs, left, was the drawing room and right, the smoking room. The gardens were much-reduced in size in later years.

Harley Street dentist Sidney Holford revs up for a ride on a motorbike in the front garden of Southernhay, 207 Hook Road, in March 1938.

Trevor Holford in the front drive of Southernhay in August 1935 with his red and cream, two-cylinder Morgan car, Rudy, just a year old. It had "magnificent acceleration but was too noisy".

Enid Blyton in 1923 during her time at Hook.

Inside the Homeware factory

Making jug mops on the factory floor.

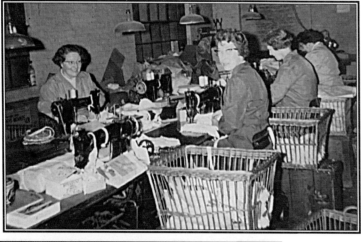

Among the workers in this upstairs factory floor. is Edith Lywood.

Time for tea: The assembly workers take a break in the staff room.

A.C. Benn's newsagents, 316 Hook Road, in the mid 1960s. Next door, there was briefly a record bar run by a Mr Nash. The next cottage, Woodstock, sold sweets.

Jeff and Carol Benn.

Duncan and Mavis Miller.

Arthur Charles Benn, born 1902, an off-licence manager at Colindale N9, saved up and opened A.C. Benn's newsagents, 311 Hook Rise, in 1936 (above, left).

After the war, he started branches at 316 and 379 Hook Road, taken over in 1979 by Preedy, then Dillons. Sons Jeff and Richard helped run the shops. At 316, Mavis Miller, an orphan from the Midlands, ran the shop with husband Duncan.

Day a strawberry was stuck in my mouth as loud train startled me

Winnie remembers Surbiton of the 1920s

WINNIE Randall moved with her family to Worthington Road, Tolworth, in 1914, at the start of the First World War. She has happy, vivid memories of Surbiton and Hook which have been cherished throughout her long life.

In her schooldays at St Matthew's, Ewell Road, the two villages were still in the countryside, which she used to explore with her two brothers.

One of the brothers, John, who is also known as Jack, also shared with his sister many reminiscences from the days of old. In April 2001, Winnie celebrated her 88th birthday at her home in The Dome, Redhill. Her brother raised a glass to his 85th birthday in April 2000 at his home in Meadowside, Sheffield.

Winnie was born in Southfields, South London, and moved as a young baby to the top flat at 34 Worthington Road, Tolworth, where her two brothers, John (Jack) and Victor were born.

Looking back over eight decades, Winnie said the 1920s were the best.

"Oh, the lovely twenties! I'm always thinking of them — so jolly and aptly named the Roaring Twenties. Will they never come back?"

With a hearty chuckle, she recalled: "One day, in the summer, when there were lovely big strawberries in season, I was walking back to Tolworth with my mother when she put a big strawberry in my mouth while we were going under the railway arch in lower Brighton Road, Surbiton.

"Suddenly a steam train clattered over and what a noise they made! I was terrified. I just stood there with the strawberry in my mouth, my eyes and mouth wide open with fright. Of course, I didn't know what it was.

"My mother said:'I wish I'd had a camera.' We were walking back to Tolworth up the Upper Brighton Road past the lovely big houses in this very select road. We went on to Kingsdowne Road and down to Ewell Road, Tolworth.

At the corner of Kingsdowne Road and Upper Brighton Road was St Bernard's School, then run by two sisters by the name of Hawkins. They were both Miss.

"Doctor Moberley's two daughters used to go, there. He used to live up Surbiton Hill in a big house called Chudleigh, which has long since been pulled down.

"I went to St Matthew's on the corner of Broomfield Road, Tolworth. It is now sadly a police station.

"The picturesque local police station on the corner of

Winnie Randall at the age of 87. In old age she treasured her childhood memories of old Tolworth and Hook.

Ellerton Road and Ditton Road, which had a blue lamp outside, has been pulled down.

"I heard from someone once that the police used our old school desks. I would love to see mine again.

"The teachers at St Matthew's were very smart and taught very well. A Miss Passey I remember very well. She lived to a ripe old age.

"I also remember a Miss Molly Peck, Miss Tranter and Miss Schofield. There used to be a teacher who was a wonderful singer and used to sing songs to us. I have wonderful memories of St Matthew's School."

The Randall siblings' mother, Edna, originally from Marden, Kent, died in November 1927 from cancer, leaving their father, jobbing gardener, Alfred, to bring them up.

Winnie Randall, her mother, and little brother Jack, in a photograph taken in Surbiton in 1917. The snapshot went to the First World War battlefields with the children's father.

Fairgrounds and Vicarage garden parties

Juicy pears from Hook

WINNIE Randall was one of the children who used to look forward each year to the summer fete held in the garden of the old Vicarage which stood opposite Hook Church, next to Orchard Court. The vicarage was demolished in 1959 but the memories of the summer festival lived on with Winnie as she approached 90 years of age.

She used to walk up what she called the "long Roman road" from the Maypole public house to Hook and then call in at the Vicarage garden parties with her school friends.

"The Vicarage was a lovely big rambling place. There was dancing on the lawn in the evening with a lovely band playing. Fairy lights were all lit up and it was lovely to watch.

"The band played all the tunes from the latest musical comedy shows — Little Nelly Kelly and No No Nanette."

She said there was entertainment from the Margaret Barnes' school of dancing and a large variety of comic sketches, too. One was very popular in the 1920s:

There was an old man who was shaving one day
He cut off his nose and exclaimed 'Oh I say, Oh I say, Oh I say'
Tut, tut, tut, Oh I say, Oh I say, Oh I say'

Winnie and her brothers used to enjoy going to a different type of fair on other occasions. It was held on waste ground close to the terraced cottages in Vale Road.

"It was great fun to watch the steam starting in the top of the roundabouts and hear the hoot as it got going. I loved to watch the little china boy in the roundabout with a black glass hat pin. He wasn't real and he would beat time to the music with a 'ching, ching ching'. He was really weird. I was afraid of him. Us children would jump onto the wooden platform as it started to go round and have a free ride. The man used to swear and shout at us to get off."

The fair was a short walk from the home of the Punchard family at 57 Thornhill Road. They were friends of Winnie's mother. Mr and Mrs Punchard's eldest child was Thomas. The middle child, Mary, died in 1921 at Surbiton Cottage Hospital aged seven from appendicitis. The couple's youngest child was called John.

Winnie lost touch with the Punchards when she moved with her family to Buckinghamshire in 1932.

She still looks back on Hook as a "dear little place" and Tolworth "with all the fields by the Red Lion public house."

She mourned the passing of Tolworth as a rural village. "We called it the country and it was. Poor Tolworth has now been pulled to pieces. My brother, John, hates the ugly Tolworth Tower and so do I."

Winnie can recall in the late summer walking up from Tolworth to work "up the wide, smooth sweep" that is Hook Road, to the fruit warehouse which became The Homeware domestic goods factory and is

Hook Road, Surbiton

The fruit store where Winnie Randall used to buy William pears is on the left and became the Homeware factory. The building was demolished in the 1960s. Budgens now trades at the site.

now demolished and replaced with Bishops, then Budgens supermarket.

"The warehouse sold these lovely William pears which were so soft and juicy. They were tuppence a pound. We got the runs because we ate so many!"

Winnie said she moved to Surbiton at the age of six months to a house in Cleaveland Road, before relocating to Tolworth a few months later.

"We had a lot of jolly times and jolly playmates in the 1920s," said Winnie. "Then we moved to Buckinghamshire in May 1932."

Living next door to the Randalls, at 32 Worthington Road was a couple called the Longhursts, who ran a hand laundry.

"My brother, Jack, used to go and get Mrs Longhurst two large bottles of ale while Mr Longhurst was out collecting washing. She used to lean over and knock on our door with a walking stick. Jack got 4d every time he went to get the ale. Mrs Longhurst called him "Jeck".

"One day, Jack got these two bottles and hung them on his bicycle handlebars. They fell off and, of course, smashed in the gutter. When my brother told Mrs Longhurst, she said: 'Quick! Go down the road and get me two more before the old man gets back. Here's sixpence.' Mr Longhurst was apparently against drinking. My brother was more careful this time for 6d was a lot of money in those days."

Choirboys in trouble

SCHOOLBOY John (Jack) Randall joined the choir of St Paul's Church, Hook, in 1925 on Ascension Day. Although he lived in Worthington Road, Tolworth, his mother, Edna, had some "very dear friends" who were members of Hook Church. He remained in the choir until 1927 when he switched to St Matthew's Church, Surbiton, where he remained for many years.

"The vicar's name then was Rev J Alban Davies", recalled John at the age of 85. "His predecessor was the Rev William Havard who became a suffragan bishop. The organist's name was Sionna Flann, an Irish gentleman who was not without a high standard of music and choir training.

"One of the choristers was Ralph Oakey, a big strapping lad, whose father owned a grocer's shop at the Vale end of Hook.

"Next to the churchyard was an orchard owned by a man named Phipps. Choirboys were to him like a red rag to a bull. Inevitably, some of the apple trees overhanging the churchyard involved using grandad's walking stick to throw up at those which were most accessible.

"Well, the inevitable happened and grandad's walking stick landed in Phipp's orchard! Of course, he was on the scene in no time and a fight of at least seven rounds took place.

"Poor Ralph sat through the choir practice with the blackest eye I have ever seen. Sionna Flann, the organist, was most sympathetic. This incident occurred in 1926.

"It was in this year, on November 5th that the parish hall was opened and I attended the ceremony.

"A further story about choir practice concerns myself and a pal. At a practice we had been singing the Le Deum, which mentions the 'Noble Army of Martyrs'. After practice, my pal Rex and I were walking through Hook Rec when we met four ex-army soldiers of the First World War. They were walking in pairs, in semi-military style with their overcoats neatly folded across their shoulders.

"Rex and I thought it good fun to join them, so we fell in behind and started singing the Noble Army of Martyrs, whereupon one of them turned round and said in no uncertain terms: 'I'll sling my b - - - - - coat at you'. I still have to smile when we sing the Le Deum.

The oak lychgate of St Paul's, given by Elizabeth Cundy in memory of James Cundy, and of Emily and Francis Clayton, of Haycroft.

St Paul's Hook, church choir in 1942 — some 15 years after the fight over apple thefts.

"I have memories of the large houses when they were occupied by one family with a staff of servants.

"The making of the Kingston bypass road completely destroyed the character of Tolworth, Hook, and Chessington. It is good to see the old photographs of how beautiful the area once was."

John had other memories of the district in his youth. In Fullers Way *(North),* there was a deep, water-filled pit called the Bluey. It was so-called, he said, because of the blue clay which was extracted to make bricks. It was a great attraction for swimming in on hot summer days.

"Legend has it that a horse and cart still lie at the bottom of the 'big Bluey' which was therefore avoided by the children; the smaller one being the one preferred. There were two 'Blueys' in the locality."

John had clear recollections of the hand laundry at 32 Worthington Road, run by the Longhursts next door to their home at No 34.

"We stood on duckboards with the water running underneath. The Longhursts employed local labour at 8d an hour. Coke stoves boiled the clothes. Close by the laundry was an allotment and irritatingly, a man would always light a bonfire which annoyed the Longhursts.

"The laundry was collected and delivered to the large houses in Surbiton and Surbiton Hill. At the top of Surbiton Hill was Tower House. At night, white owls used to fly around the towers. As children, we used to call them ghosts.

"Mr Aggas was the bootmaker in Hook Road *(close to Haycroft Road)* and his son used to help him.

"My mother, who died in 1927, used to help the Punchard family who lived in Thornhill Road. She would do jobs for them in the house. The Punchards then moved to Somerset Avenue."

John recalls a Mrs Constance Fathers who lived at Ditton Dene, (now 55 Hook Road), a double-fronted house close to the junction of Thornhill Road. He said: "Mrs Fathers was the organist at Oaklands Baptist Church, Surbiton Hill, She always wore a red hat. The pipe organ is no longer there.

"Hook had a very good social life in those days. There was this gimmick where people became 'The Mayor of Hook'. It was a charity event to raise money to build the parish hall.

"Hook and Southborough was a model parish in those days."

Scarlet fever claimed couple's only son

Shirley and the neighbours

GWENDOLEN Freeman's name can be added to the impressive list of authors who have lived in Hook Road and helped put it on the map. She spent her girlhood at Shirley, 62 Hook Road and after leaving the district for a career in journalism on the Birmingham Post, returned to live at 416 Hook Road in 1948.

In the summer of 2001, while in her early nineties, this remarkably resilient resident was still working as a newspaper columnist, contributing articles for publications all over the country. Furthermore, she was preparing a new book to add to the long list of her published works, many of which look at family life in the first part of the century, not just in the Surbiton area but in the Midlands, too.

And Gwendolen's sister, Barbara, who lived at Shirley, until her death in 1999 at the age of 93, was also involved in the world of books. For a time she was an illustrator for Enid Blyton. Sadly, her old home was set ablaze in the early summer of 2001 by squatters who moved into the house — the most southerly of the four terraced villas built in the late 1850s and were known then as Southborough Terrace. (Two of the villas became Shirley and Netley named after Southampton suburbs by an occupant from the city a century ago).

Miss Freeman, who remained single throughout her long-life, but adopted two boys, gave an interview to Mark Davison in April 2000 at her home in Hook Road.

She spoke colourfully of the Hook Road she knew in her schooldays at Tiffins, Kingston, at the time of the First World War.

"Then it was like living in the middle of the country," she said. "I was born in Ealing. My father, William Freeman, was a journalist who had a bookshop. I was three when we came out here *(to Hook)*. My grandfather was also called William Freeman and he ran an art shop near Surbiton Station in Victoria Terrace. My father stood twice as a Liberal MP candidate but he lost his deposit both times."

Next door to Shirley at what is now 60 Hook Road, was Netley, occupied by the Pryor family. Frederick and Emily Pryor had seven children. Miss Freeman remembers tragedy striking when the youngest boy, Jimmy, died at the age of about seven from scarlet fever.

"It was an awful shock," she said. "He died at home." Gwendolen and Barbara used to wheel the youngest of the Pryor children down the Hook Road in a pram and play with the older brothers and sisters. She remembers Mr Pryor as having "a reddish face".

Next door to Netley, at what is now 58 Hook Road was the villa Normanshurst. Here, Ernest and Clara Kyte resided in the early 1920s.

"Mr Kyte was rather like Mr Punch in the Punch and Judy shows," said Miss Freeman. "He worked at Bumps, a famous bookshop in London. They got on well with my father. In the end they went to Canada and he became a librarian. He married again and by then had had three wives. He was quite a character. He was very good to me and at one stage intended to publish some of my memoirs."

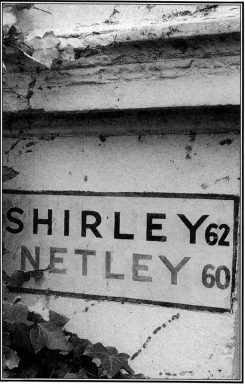

The Freeman family from Shirley, Hook Road, in about 1916. They are pictured in the garden of family friend, Harold Long at Heasleigh, 239 Hook Road, opposite the parish hall. Pictured with parents, Lucy and William Freeman, are their children, left to right, Barbara, Peter, Gwendolen and Rosemary. Peter, who went to Kingston Grammar School, died at the age of 16. Following a smallpox scare, he was kept in Tolworth Hospital for months, sent home saying "he'd be all right by the new year" and developed scarlet fever. It proved fatal. The Shirley sign on the gate pillars survived to the 21st century. In the summer of 2001, the fire-damaged Shirley was sold for more than £300,000.

Living next door, in a large old Victorian house called Ravenshurst, on the south side of the terrace, was Dr Robert Archibald Macneill and his wife, Ida. Their home was pulled down in the early 1960s and The Clifton maisonettes now occupy the site.

"Robert Macneill was a very silent doctor. He would stand looking at you and therefore he got a reputation. We respected him. He was a silent Scot. He gave us books. We were poor and they used to feed their dogs on chocolate which we thought terrible. Mrs Macneill was quiet, too, and her sister lived with them. They seemed frightfully good. We were in awe of them. They gave us a copy of Wind In The Willows. He was there when I had my tonsils out. He was a big man."

Dr Richard Archibald Mowll — an austere man with a black moustache — and his wife, Sarah Myra Mowll, lived further down the Hook Road at No 14, then known as Derrynane and now No 20.

The Freeman girls were also friendly with the daughters of Nellie and William Page who lived at Watersmeet, now 51 Hook Road.

Said Gwendolen: "They had two girls who went to Surbiton High and they seemed superior to us. One was dark, one was fair. It was a grand, paying school."

The Benneys — Henry and Elizabeth — resided at Melinda, now 59 Hook Road. Mr Benney was "a bit of a clown" and "they came to our parties. They had two children who went to Tiffins. Muriel, the elder girl, went on to work for the local council."

Lucy Freeman's parents, Rosetta and George Lydster Rimmington, lived close by at Vellmead, Ditton Road. Mr Rimmington was a sidesman at St Matthew's Church. Lucy had been a head girl at Tiffins.

...old villas in Hook

THERE was only one room heated in the Freemans' Victorian villa when daughter Gwendolen was a young girl. The four children would huddle around the coal fire in the sitting room of Shirley, ...ok Road, and would quarrel that there wasn't enough space. Brother ...er would be accused of taking up too much room with his knees.

...n her book, A Zeppelin In My Childhood, (Tallis Press 1987) ...endolen Freeman draws a graphic picture of life at the time the ...4-18 war broke out.

...One of my chief memories of childhood is of the cold — freezing ...ks in fog which we do not have today; cold in under-heated rooms; ...ering cold in bed with unheated bedrooms and one stone hot ...er bottle between all of us.

...n most homes in winter, there was only one fire — in the sitting ...m. The rest of the house was left to nature except for the 'range' or ...stove in the kitchen, and each winter pipes froze and then burst and ...home water was rationed or cut off for days.

...Those smoky little fires brought the discomfort of dirt as well. Each ...se had its black coal shed or coal bunker. Coal scuttles had to be

Nos 53 and 55 Hook Road (formerly numbered 47 and 49) — Ranmoor and Ditton Dene. The organist at Oaklands Baptist Church, Constance Fathers lived at Ditton Dene in the 1920s.

Melinda, formerly no 53 and now 59 Hook Road. Here the Freeman sisters from Shirley, over the road, made friends with the Benney family in the 1920s. Mr Benney was "a bit of a clown".

...nny Chisholm, outside Stormont, Southborough ...Terrace, now 56 Hook Road, in the summer of ...001 by which time he had lived in the villa for ...ore than 35 years. He has been actively involved ...with the Hook Leisure Gardens Association. The ...eemans occupied the furthest villa, damaged by ... fire in 2001 after squatters started a blaze.

filled and carried in and set by the hearths. My mother said later that I was a dirty baby and liked eating coal. Few babies today, in the South at least, would have a chance of eating it.

"When we were quite young, we began to look after the hearth. It had a poker, shovel and brush, tongs, a toasting fork and 'dogs' on which to lean some of the furnishings. In front of the grate was the draw plate which had to be taken out so that you could sweep out the ashes from underneath.

"You removed all the furnishings, swept out the ashes, and then washed the tiles with a wet rag, making a 'dirty' smell.

"There might be a brass fender which had to be cleaned and the hearth furnishings often had brass in them which also needed cleaning. Otherwise they were polished with black lead. It made hours of work.

"We also had to buy bundles of wood, or chop wood to start the fire each day. Finally the sweep would come, generally in the spring. He hadn't a vacuum those days but scraped away with his brushes and the soot came down in clouds. We had covered up the room as far as we could beforehand but there had to be a thorough cleaning afterwards. Sitting by the fire in the winter, your cheeks would burn but your back would still be frozen.

"We had, of course, only cold water from our taps and taps only in the kitchen and bath-

Barbara, Peter, Gwendolen and Rosemary Freeman in about 1916.

room. In our house, a dull old geyser with a pilot light heated water for our weekly baths, but it seemed frequently to go wrong or be said to be dangerous and it made a frightening explosion when it was lit.

"In the kitchen was a great copper in a corner with old apparatus for boiling clothes, but we used it for preserving eggs in treacly waterglass and got our hot water by kettles and zinc baths on the gas stove. Clothes were not easy to wash. They shrank and went hard.

"There were no detergents, only soap which mixed badly with our hard London water. Shirts had to be starched with added 'bluebag'. You made the starch in a basin by pouring boiling water on to a solution of white powder, and it became gluey and grey. Little girls' frocks, adults' aprons and cuffs all had to be starched, and with the long laundering process, were not washed as often. One put on clean clothes once a week — on Sundays. There were no zips in those days but many tapes and buttons. We wore more garments and shoes were stiffer. Dressing was arduous each day, especially in cold bedrooms. But summer had its trials too, with flies, nourished by the horse manure in the streets, buzzing against the window panes or trapped and feebly dying on long strips of sticky paper in the kitchen. We knew nothing of fly sprays. House cleaning methods were primitive. We had only a sweeper which failed to pick up all the crumbs."

Haven soup kitchen

TWO elderly ladies who were born and brought up in the Southborough part of Hook in the 1890s relived their memories in the presence of a local newspaper historian in 1973. As Christmas approached that year, the two members of Hook Over 60s Club turned back the clock while Margaret Bellars, of the Kingston Borough News, took down their story.

Thankfully, their reminiscences can be re-told because Kingston Local History Centre, part of Kingston Museum, has kept bound copies of the Borough News from that time.

Miss Evelyn Franklin was born at 2 Clare Cottages, St James Road, Southborough. That was the address when her parents moved into today's Brook Road, Hook, in 1889. Her next-door neighbour at the detached Lynn Cottage, next to the mission hall, was John Stickley. When she celebrated her 80th birthday in December 1973 she was living at 16 Haycroft Road, Hook, (formerly Crosby, or Crossley Cottages), just round the corner from her birthplace.

The 1891 census, which was not available for public viewing at the time of the 1973 interview, reveals that Berkshire-born Alfred Franklin, a fishmonger's assistant aged 30, was living with his Dorking-born wife, Esther, 27, at the cottage that year. No children are listed at that time.

Margaret Bellars' interview takes up the story. Eventually, the Franklins had five children, all of whom went to school at St Paul's, Orchard Road, Hook.

One of Evelyn's schoolfriends and a life-long soulmate was Mrs Connie Brown, born in 1899, who in retirement lived at 4, Brook Road, Hook. Mrs Brown, as a girl, lived in Orchard Road, then a muddy lane. She was one of nine children.

Evelyn started going to school at the age of two years and four months.

"They were happy days — more than they are now," she said. "Everyone was so friendly. We made our own fun."

She said that Hook was really in the country then. There were hardly any street lights. There was a lamp near St Bernard's School, (now 19 Upper Brighton Road, Surbiton) and then no more lights along the main road until Leatherhead.

"We used to travel by horse-buses. Both sides of the road had deep ditches and high hedges. It was very scaring to walk after dark."

In the Orchard Road area it was much the same.

"We had only a few street lamps. The lamplighter used to come night and morning," said Mrs Brown. "There was plenty of interest.

"On Sundays, the muffin man would come round ringing his bell. In the summer, 'Catch-em Alive,' the flypaper man came round wearing flypapers on his top hat.

"There was also the watercress man and an old chap everyone called Happy Jack. He sold honeysuckle plants. He lived in the woods

Evelyn Franklin, left, and Connie Brown, reminiscing in 1973 about their girlhood days in Hook.

behind the present Chessington Zoo. We kids used to run away when we saw him."

Counting up, Mrs Brown and Miss Franklin found they had been in the parish of Hook under 11 vicars. Miss Franklin sang in the choir when Mr Peter Jeal was organist. He later went on to Thames Ditton Church, she recalled.

A centre of social life, and welfare, in the area was The Haven Coffee Rooms and Working Men's Club, with Mr George Ive, manager and secretary.

The Haven, (now 168 and 170 Hook Road — I.L.Brock Co, insurance brokers and the showrooms of Chessington Motorcycles) was opened in 1885 as a charity-run concern, managed by the vicar and churchwardens of St Paul's Church. It is understood there were earlier coffee rooms at the premises which had closed down prior to the pair of semi-detached Victorian cottages being bought by Robert Norton-Stevens with £500 he raised from parishioners' and his own donations. Mr Norton-Stevens lived in the 1870s at Southborough Terrace, Hook Road (opposite Thornhill Road junction) and later at The Rhodrons (Rhodrons Avenue).

The Haven had to be run "for purposes in connection with the parish . . .as a place of meeting and association, for purposes of Christian instruction, mental improvement and culture, and for refreshment — not including alcoholic drink — and recreation." Religious teaching would be provided on Sundays.

When Connie and Evelyn cast their minds back, The Haven was the local slate club premises. The men had a club under Mr Ive. His wife ran a women's slate club.

It was also the place where the Girls' Friendly Society (forerunner of the Girls Brigade) held their meetings and where the Misses Dickie and Newton taught Bible classes and where useful crafts were learned.

But above all, The Haven was where it was possible to get a night's

The former Haven coffee rooms and soup kitchen, now 168 & 170 Hook Road.

lodging "on the parish" for 2d, including a supper of bread cheese and cocoa, plus a good breakfast the following morning.

In addition, it was one of two soup kitchens in the area. At Haven, a large ewer jug of hot soup cost just 2d (less than 1p).

Connie's family from Orchard Road and Evelyn's from St Jam Road were among the clients.

Said Connie: "It was lovely soup. Thick and rich, made from ple of good meat. We used to come down and fetch it twice a wee the Haven and twice a week at the parish hall."

Connie's father was a gardener. For a time he worked at Ennad the house which stood on the corner of Orchard Road and H Road and where Harry Hawker, the famous aviator lived. W Connie's father worked there, it was owned by one of the daugh of Marie Lloyd. She had married a jockey, Edgar Wheatley. W Marie Lloyd was appearing at Kingston Empire, she used to sta the Albany Hotel, Thames Ditton, Mrs Brown said. Marie did a lo shopping in Kingston Market.

Oakey's

GENERATIONS of Hook families will have memories of Oakey's Stores. The grocer's was run from 1, St Mary's Villas, Hook Road, Southborough, for more than half a century by the Oakey family.

The business was started by Leonard and Ethel Oakey, originally from Alvescott, Oxon, and later taken on by their son, Harold, and his wife, Mabel, (Mabs) with whom he was married for 64 years.

The store traded from what is today 140 Hook Road — in the year 2001 a print shop.

St Mary's Villas were built in 1883 and are in the Hook Road between Gladstone and Brook Roads.

Harold was actively involved with the 1st Hook Scout Group all his life. He was a past president of Kingston District Grocers' Federation and Master of Kingston Temple Lodge. He was also a governor of the Royal Masonic Hospital.

His memory will live on in the scouts' Oakey awards, presented to scouts who are good team members and live by "Oakey's rules".

Harold was father to Elizabeth and Marjorie and at the time of his death was grandfather to Warren, Charlotte, Denise and Lorraine, and great-grandfather to Jessica and Alice.

Leonard's other son, Ralph, ran a shop at Berrylands, near the Bun Shop.

Mabel Oakey, wife of Harold, the proprietor's son, pictured with a grocery assistant and Ethel Oakey, wife of Leonard, at the shop at No 140 (formerly 116) Hook Road, Hook, which the family ran from the early 1920s to 1979. Leonard had previously opened up a provisions store at Wimbledon before the First World War. This photograph was taken in the late 1930s. The shop became in 1959 one of the first self-service supermarkets in Surbiton and was as big a concern as the Sainsbury's store at Ace Parade. The store was sold in 1979 but Harold Oakey remained the owner for a time until a Mr Patel bought the business from him. After its closure some years later, it became a print shop. Harold (inset) died on 18th July 2000 aged 92.

...el, Leonard and Ralph, c1912.

Old Victorian mansion pulled down — flats built on the site

St Bernard's School (Southborough Lodge)

End of year prizegiving, c1956. Lynn Holford receives a cup from Miss Sparks.

Garth Holford's children, John and Lynn at St Bernard's sports d

SAINT Bernard's Preparatory School for Girls moved from the top of the Upper Brighton Road, junction with Kingsdowne Road, in the 1940s to Southborough Lodge, an eight-bedroomed house at 54 Hook Road (formerly no 32).

Southborough Lodge was built about 1872 for military boot and shoemaker, John Kerby. Born in 1821 in Wiltshire, Mr Kerby for several years beforehand lived next door at Fairfield, now 38 Hook Road — next to Ash Tree Close — and one of the oldest villas still standing in the main street.

The Kerbys were a family very set in their ways.

After John's death, his son John (Jack) Ramsey Kerby continued to live at the property for many years with his family.

In the 1920s, the house had long rooms illuminated by ornate chandelier lights. Fields at the back of the house spread out to Shrewsbury House School. Friends and family arrived in summer to cut the hay and the event turned into quite a harvest-time party.

The Kerbys were among the last people in Surbiton to change their personal transport from a horse and carriage to a motor car. They kept

two horses in stables tended to by coachman and groom, Mr Putt

Jack's nephew, Garth Holford, then living in Uxbridge R Kingston, as a child remembered going to Southborough Lodge t taken to the cinema in the horse and carriage with his Aunt "C Kerby, his father's sister.

"You'd hear a patter of hooves and they brought the coach r to the front in the semi-circular drive. If we were good, we could with Mr Puttock in the front in the box."

Garth's aunt was a little suspicious. At Christmas, when the fa of 13 gathered for a festive lunch, she would make sure there were not 13 seats together, so she sat at a little extra table with an inch between her and the relatives.

Jack Kerby used to be a keen member of the Surbiton Club in St James' Road. Young Garth used to meet him there on occasions in the early 1920s. Once Garth discovered a letter addressed to his uncle at the club. As a favour he deemed it a good idea to personally take the letter to his uncle's home at Southborough Lodge.

The reaction from his uncle who received the letter could not have been predicted. He was furious.

"He told me it was a private letter and I got a hell of a ticking off. That's why it was sent to the club and not his home," Garth recalled.

St Bernard's School in its Hook Road location was run in the best traditions of the day by the Misses Bolley and Sparks. End-of-year prizegiving was attended by parents in the rear garden, weather permitting, near a giant rhododendron — bright red in spring — and the shade of a huge cedar tree.

Sports day in the Shrewsbury House School fields was made fun for all. First there was a procession around the field, smallest children firmly in hand by the older ones. Events covered all age groups and included tiny visitors, whose older sisters were traditionally able to persuade their siblings to run faster by pushing or pulling. There were prizes for parents' races and for home-made hats.

For many years in the first part of the 20th century, the villa next door to Southborough Lodge was referred to as Sungate. It refers to half of the old pair of Victorian semis which was still standing at the start of the 21st century, and which is now 38 Hook Road.

In the 1920s, the five-bedroomed Sungate was owned by the Betteley family. Alice and Edward Betteley lived there for several years between the two world wars.

In 1914, with a rateable value of £750, Sungate was one of the most desirable properties in the road, having a higher figure than each of the villas in the neighbouring Southborough Terrace.

The old Southborough Lodge which was used as a school, St Bernard's, in the 1930s and 1950s. In the early days at Hook Road, after moving from Upper Brighton Road, it took boys and girls. Later it served as a preparatory school just for girls.

The old coach-house for Southborough Lodge, now no. 42 Hook Road and hidden by tall gates, was in 2000 put on the market for an asking price of £600,000. It has been greatly extended over the years.

Southborough Lodge was pulled down in the early 1960s and was replaced with St Bernard's House flats. Kingston Council has put tree preservation orders on the lime, ash, fastigate and hornbeam trees in the grounds.

Fairfield – or Fairfields (36 Hook Road) — forms a pair of 1860s, or slightly earlier, three-storey semis. For a time in its early existence, one half of the pair appears to have been called Southborough Villa.

When John Kerby snr moved out in the early 1870s, Jane Norton and her family, from Scole, Norfolk, moved in and remained for many years. Mrs Norton was born in 1810 and was a widow. Living with her were grown-up spinster daughters Luisa, Rose and Jane as well as her son, Fred. They had two servants who carried out the cooking duties and general chores. Mrs Norton died in 1896.

St Bernard's House, 54 Hook Road — the name of the flats recalls the old school on the site.

Sungate and Fairfield, 38&36 Hook Road, date back to the 1860s.

Family's long link with Surbiton and Hook

The Farmers

FOR more than 120 years the Farmer family have been linked to Hook, Southborough and Surbiton. This remarkable span began when John Farmer arrived in Surbiton in 1880 with his wife, Ann, and started running a butcher's shop at 126 Ewell Road.

The couple had six children when they arrived and two more were born during those early Surbiton years. Mrs Farmer had hailed from Thorpe, near Egham, and previously Mr Farmer had run a butcher's at Guildford High Street.

Their third child was William, and as he grew older, he took over the butcher's from his father, changing the business name from J. Farmer to W.B. Farmer. William later married Sybil Newton, widowed in 1912.

A letter sent to John Farmer in 1917.

Ann and John Farmer who arrived in Surbiton in 1880 and moved to 89 Ewell Road in 1898.

In 1907, William bought Brook Farm at Southborough off Miss Selfe, who lived opposite at a house called Southborough Hill. Brook Farm's two fair-sized farm cottages stood roughly where the modern day Edward Pinner Court is sited. The farm had four acres of land on which in later years were built the newer sections of Haycroft, Gladstone, Brook Road and Herne Roads.

In the late 1920s, the farm had a granary next to the cottages which had wooden steps going up to a corn store. Mr Farmer kept one cow, a number of chickens, pigs and about 10 white geese. A stream ran through the meadows and the geese fiercely guarded the property, which dated back to at least the 1860s.

Mr Farmer never lived at the farm but saw it as an investment. He enjoyed strolling up the rural Hook Road on a stifling hot summer's afternoon to enjoy the open countryside and "refreshing breeze" after a sweltering day in the butcher's at Ewell Road. This reference to the gusts of wind may have been the reason behind a property almost opposite the farm being called Sea Breeze Cottage. Mr Farmer sold off the farmland in the early 1930s for redevelopment and owned the freehold of 32 houses in Gladstone Road, 34 in Haycroft and six in both Brook and Hook Roads. He had one

child, William John, from his marriage to Sybil, who already had three children, Sybil, John and Kathy. Son William, born 1918, lived for four years in the late 1920s at Herne Road with his parents. When his mother died there in 1929, he moved with his grandmother and aunts to the house Baynards, 89 Ewell Road, Surbiton Hill, which had been in the family since 1898. He was still living there in 2001 and had only in recent years retired from managing his father's Southborough properties, now in a trust. His father died in 1945 aged 73.

Sybil Farmer, wife of William B Farmer, with baby son, William John Farmer, in 1919.

William B Farmer.

Tiny William & half siblings.

Baynards, 89 Ewell Road — in Farmer family since 1898.

William John Farmer, still living at Baynards, Ewell Road, in 2001.

Florrie Wiltshire in the fields at Brook Farm, Hook Road, Southborough, with a young family friend, Nina Ratcliffe, who was visiting from Epsom. Miss Wiltshire lived for much of her life at 18 Vale Road South until the great flood of July 6th 1973 rendered her terraced home uninhabitable. She lived to the age of 94. Her niece, Pam Neame, in 2001 was living in Kent Way.

Escapee goat found hanged by tether

Fields of daisies and cows

CHARLES and Mary Wiltshire lived at Brook Farm, Hook Road, during the Second World War. Charles was a carter, working with horses at Stickley's yard next to what is now Southborough School. Mary was a nature lover and took in all the waifs and strays of the animal world. Many times her daughter, Pam, would find a box in the hearth carrying abandoned fledglings.

There was an outdoor toilet and no bathroom at their farm cottage at 112 Hook Road (now replaced by Edward Pinner Court). The pair of semi-detached cottages dated back to at least 1860. In the war years, food was cooked on a Kitchener fire which Mr Wiltshire later moved to the garden so pig swill could be cooked. The Wiltshires kept a small farm of a dozen pigs, geese, and rabbits, which the family bred. At Christmas time, daughter Pam would pluck geese ready for cooking for the festive table. Cooking apples were sold to Mr Cheshire for sale in his shop at nearby Vale Terrace. In the fields were daisies and a brook. A goat kept by the family used to escape frequently. Once it was found wandering up Herne Road by Dennis Stickley who raised the alarm. Then, tragedy struck. The goat climbed onto an air raid shelter, fell off and hung itself from its tether.

Left: Charles Wiltshire, a carter, who lived with his family at Brook Farm Cottages in the early 1940s. He is pictured with a horse in the farm fields.

Right: A family snapshot taken outside the cowshed at Brook Farm. Top right is Charles Wiltshire. Bottom right is Mrs Mary Wiltshire. Top left is Gordon Marshall, a half-brother of Pam Wiltshire, pictured bottom left.

Lawrence's, the butcher's, 172 Hook Road — now a DIY store

The butcher's goes up for auction in 1930.

The DIY shop which was trading in the year 2001 at 172 Hook Road, Hook.

D O-IT-YOURSELF enthusiasts buying paint, rawlplugs or shelves at the PRW store, 172 Hook Road, probably have no inkling that once the premises was a butcher's.

But if you get into a long conversation with the shopkeeper when he is not taking money for sandpaper, brooms or wheelie-bins, he will explain that at the rear of the store, there are still some clues.

These are some old butcher's hooks still hanging in a dark corner.

They are the only evidence that for more than 40 years, from the late 1880s to 1930, this was the main butcher's shop serving Hook. In the 1890s it was run by William Turner and his son, John. By the 1920s, William and Louisa Lawrence were running the business.

Reg Driver was born at 8 Haycroft Road on 9th June 1919. As an 82-year-old he recalled 'Slacky' Lawrence as "a fat man with straw hat wearing a blue and white striped apron, sharpening his knives."

In those days, the shop had a different number — 142 Hook Road — and it is probable that before numbering started along the road, in about 1918, the premises was called Crossley House.

The former butcher's shop, yard and coachhouse in the year 2001.

The shop stood in a prominent position on the corner of Hook Road and Haycroft Road.

A yard at the back stretched down some 85ft and at the end, before the double-fronted cottage, was the butcher's coach house with a stable for the housing of one horse. Above it was a loft. The Lawrences had kept their meat cool by means of storage in an ice safe.

In February 1930, the shop, house and business went up for sale. By this time, Mrs Lawrence was on her own and obviously found it too much to cope with.

The house had at that time two bedrooms at the front on the first floor and another bedroom at the rear, facing Haycroft Road. There was also a semi-basement at garden level in which was a kitchen with a range, copper and sink. Like other Victorian homes nearby, the toilet was outside.

The old Southborough Arms stood on the opposite corner, just a few yards away.

Nos 1 & 2 William's Cottages, (26 & 28) Haycroft Road, in 2001. The name brick has been half covered by rendering applied to No 28 so their original name can only be worked out from other clues. The neighbouring cottages at Nos 18-24 were known as South West Cottages, homes in the 1890s to two young railway porters from Hants and Dorset.

What a muddle the address of Haycroft Road has been over the years. When first developed more than a century ago, it was known as Southborough Road, Southborough, Surbiton, or Southborough Road, Hook. It then became Haycroft Road, Hook, Surbiton, as it is now. To add to the earlier confusion, another Southborough Road was being constructed near The Maypole. Furthermore, some people called Hook Road 'Southborough Road' in Victorian times.

The butcher's neighbours to the rear lived at Surbiton Cottages, nos 2, 4 and 6 Haycroft Road, built in about 1873. The pretty double-fronted cottage at no2 has the brick-built butcher's stable adjoining it. The terrace downhill (nos 8-16) was known as Crossley Cottages and dates back to before 1880.

Homes for farm labourers, cowmen, and washer women in Victorian times

Haycroft Road

HAYCROFT Road was so-named because it adjoined Haycroft Farm and land belonging to Haycroft House in Hook. The first cottages in this little street provided much-needed accommodation for the many labourers, farm workers and men employed across the Hook Road at the Southborough brickfields. The brickworks was operating just south of Verona Drive but by the 1890s had closed.

In 1881, the terraced row of homes called Crosby, or Crossley, Cottages had an assortment of people living there. James May lived in the first cottage, later 28 Haycroft Road. Born in Dorking in 1836, he was an agricultural worker, along with his wife, Charlotte, who was a year older, and their son, Alfred, aged 18. Another son, Frederick, aged 14, had already left school and was working as a farm carter.

The couple's other two sons, Walter, aged nine, and Arthur aged four, both born in Hook, were still at school. Their cottage would have been quite basic with an outside WC.

The Mays' next-door neighbour, Henry Novell, aged 40 was a general labourer who had a wife and eight children to bring up. Two sons,

Henry and Aldred, were already employed as labourers to help bring some much-needed money into the household to feed the hungry mouths.

At 3 Crosby Cottages (12 Haycroft Road) lived James Turner, 47, a brick labourer. He and his wife, Martha, helped make ends meet by taking in lodgers. The two boarders both worked in the brickfields, one as a burner.

Another brick labourer, William Lazell, 55, lived next door. His wife earned some extra housekeeping working as a charwoman.

Mr Lazell's likely colleagues, Charles Laremore, 36, and his wife were also employed at the brickworks and lived at the end of the terrace. They had a son and four daughters fighting for space at the home. Most of the householders could only afford to rent their homes.

The brickfields have gone but in 2001, the terrace still provided homes for local people like Mrs Nash who lived at No 8 for many years. One of her modern day errand 'boys' was Reg Driver who was born at the house in 1919.

Cottages owned by William Farmer had rents as low as £7 a week until recent years; the level being set many years ago. This has been quoted as the reason so many people stayed in the road so long.

Landlord and wife had 13 children

Southborough Arms

THE Southborough Arms used to stand at the corner of Hook Road and Haycroft Road but when the Kingston bypass was built in the late 1920s, there were plans to move the public house to a more prominent position. The new Southborough Arms was opened in the 1930s next to the new bypass road. In recent times it was run by Wetherspoons and was called The Cap in Hand.

Back in the 1880s, the Southborough Arms was a new pub on the Hook Road and catered for the many labourers living or working around the new Haycroft Road, Gladstone Road, Brook Road, and Vale Road developments.

The "spit and sawdust" hostelry also sold some meat and groceries. It was then run by Matthew Stickley and his wife, Amelia, from Deptford, "Kent", who he married in 1870. Their first marital home was at 3 Vale Place, Hook Road (the terraced cottages later known as Vale Terrace, just north of Vale Road North.)

Matthew Stickley was born in Wareham, Dorset, in about 1849, and was one of nine children. He was the youngest son of James Stickley and Jane Davis, who married in 1828 and had nine children in their Dorset household. Matthew was a dairyman before he took over the Southborough Arms.

The licensed victualler couple had 13 children, Emma, Horace, Amelia, William, Ernest, Herbert Oliver, Herbert Charles, Florence, Douglas, Mable, Julia, Percy, John and Gladys.

Amelia, a twin; William, and Julia did not survive, however. Some of the other offspring moved later in life to Canada and Stickley descendants still live in the Vancouver area.

One of Matthew and Amelia's sons, Percy Walter, born in 1886, died during the First World War, possibly in May 1916 while serving with the Royal Navy on HMS Black Prince.

The Stickleys remained friends with people in Dorset and visitors from the county sometimes stayed at Hook.

The 1891 census reveals that the Stickleys were still the pub's landlords. Daughter, Emma, was by now a 19-year-old "teacher of pianoforte" while Horace was a dairyman's assistant.

A century later, Ormonde Joinery Products occupied the former hostelry at what in modern times is 174 Hook Road.

The former Southborough Arms, Hook Road, in the year 2001.

An artist's impression of Hook Road, Southborough, as it was in 1922, drawn by Rex Houle, of Clayton Road, Hook, in 1978.

A leaded window from the old Southborough Arms pub is now in the safekeeping of Mark Davison's Hook archives collection. He purchased the window in 1992.

This picture is taken from a postcard produced a few years after the 1939-45 war. But it is the wording on the back which is equally as interesting as the view. It was sent by schoolgirl Eileen Hornshaw, then of 50 Haycroft Road, to a friend in Australia. She states: "The shop marked 'X' is where we post all our mail — the Hook Post Office in fact. Notice the television ariel's (sic) 'H'. Have you ever seen T.V.? We have one — have had it for four years now." The post office was soon to move from Enfield House down the road next to the Tip Top cafe. In recent years Hook Road Post Office closed. Middleton's Laundry buildings are next to the then new parade.

Haycroft Road

1940s

EILEEN Hornshaw, now Mrs Gould, was born at 50 Haycroft Road in 1937. Her parents had moved to Hook from Battersea "to get away from the pollution," and because her sister was frail "and needed fresh air."

Hook was still then in the countryside. At the bottom of Haycroft Road was a swamp common on which lived a family of Romany gipsies.

The gipsies lived in an old-style caravan which was beautifully furnished behind the engraved glass doors.

The gipsy couple were known to the children in the road as Mr and Mrs Dixie, but this may not have been their real name.

They cooked on open fires and boiled water in a "big old pot" hung over the embers.

Their caravan was immaculately kept. It was full of brasses and shiny objects.

Mrs Dixie wore long, black, ankle-length clothes and an apron. Her husband was "a lovely man" according to Eileen. "Very swarthy."

The children accompanied the gipsies to Kingston Market

An end-of-war street party at Haycroft Road, Hook, in 1945.

where they took their hay and rode in the empty cart on its return.

The marshy land behind Haycroft Road was formerly known as Hook Hearn Common. Hence Herne Road, extended in the 1930s from Ditton Hill to Hook Road.

The Romanies travelled around in the horse-drawn cart and the Dixies enjoyed giving the youngsters rides to and from the elm tree-bordered meadow.

The gipsies showed some of the local girls how to make pegs using willow.

The gipsies could not read or write very well and people living in the houses at the bottom of Haycroft Road used to read out documents and fill in forms for them.

Around the time of the Second World War, the residents of Gladstone and Haycroft Roads used coupons to purchase household items because rationing was in force.

Eileen recalled that her mother, Violet, was poor and always ran up a slate so she could pay when she could afford to. Her father, Edward, worked as an electrician.

Families used to go into Oakey's stores at St Mary's Terrace, Hook Road, for their groceries or walk up the road to the Sainsbury's supermarket at Ace Parade, opened on July 2nd 1938, and watch butter being patted into shape.

They could also buy cheap broken biscuits at Sainsbury's.

Eileen attended St Paul's School and was taught by Miss Joan Rumble and Mr Fred Clark.

At weekends in winter, if the weather was cold, the water in the meadows on the common used to freeze over and the boys and girls would skate on the ice.

Eileen said her parents rented their house from a Mr Farmer who owned quite a few properties in the neighbourhood. The Farmer family ran Brook Farm and a W B Farmer sold meat from a butcher's at Ewell Road, Surbiton, in the Edwardian years.

Hook vicar, Rev John Selwyn Taborn, who took up the post only the previous year, is seated next to Eileen Hornshaw — dressed as a gipsy — at the VE day celebration street party in Haycroft Road, Hook, in 1945.

VE day celebrations in Gladstone Road, 1945

Celebrating the end of the Second World War with a VE day street party in Gladstone Road, Hook. The terrace of nine cottages, still standing, was known as Alderstone Cottages. — now No 4-10 & 16-24.

DURING the Second World War, in 1944, a doodlebug landed on commonland at the rear of Kelvin Grove and went off, shattering windows in Haycroft Road. Parts of No 50 Haycroft Road, built in the 1930s, were damaged but Vi and Ted Hornshaw and their children escaped injury by hiding in a Morrison shelter constructed indoors.

The shelter was huge and took up most of the Hornshaws' kitchen-dining room space and had to double up as a table for the family.

Some 55 years later, Eileen Hornshaw recalled the war: "I can remember standing at the back door watching the search lights criss-crossing the night sky, lighting up a German plane. I think it got shot down," she said.

"My father couldn't go to war because being an electrician with the London Electricity Board, he was a reserved occupation. He served his country by being in the Home Guard and was sent to an airfield in Pembrokeshire. It meant we saw him more often than the children whose fathers went to war, which was nice.

"He used to cycle to Battersea to his place of work, mostly down the A3. If he had a bit of cash spare, he put his bike on the train at Raynes Park, but that was rare.

"Most of my parents' relatives still lived in London at the time but after the war my cousins, Pat and Dennis, who lived in a council flat in Wandsworth, used to spend school holidays with us and Oh! What fun we used to have. They thought we lived in the country and they loved it.

"My mother was easy going and never really got cross with us. All the kids loved her. One of our games was jumping the ditches, more often than not falling in but my mum used to dry the kids out before they went home. Playing marbles in the gutter and five stones — dabs — passed away lots of time. Living in a cul-de-sac, which backed onto commonland, orchards and cornfields was a child's delight.

"We used to make underground dens digging down about three or four feet, building the sides up with turf and old bits of corrugated iron for the roof. What could be better? The swamps on the common meant we learnt a lot about nature. There were newts, tadpoles and frogs.

"Mrs Gadd at no60 Haycroft Road used to supply the gipsies with water. My mum also helped them with documents but couldn't understand why they couldn't write. I used to play with the Dixies' grand-daughter, Patience, when she visited. Regarding those pegs, Mrs Dixie broke off the young willow branches, stripped off the soft bark and cut them to size using a template. A piece of soft metal was then put around one end and secured with a nail. The other end was slit down the middle with a sharp knife and a slither of wood removed."

The open countryside before Woodgate Avenue and Devon Way were built

CHRISTINE Vann's first memory of Newlands Way, Hook, was December 1939 when her parents and two small sisters moved from Derek Avenue, West Ewell. In those days there were just eight houses at the lower end of the road and a few bungalows and houses at the top. Although her childhood was spent mostly during the war years she enjoyed many happy times, in spite of the bombs, doodlebugs, food rationing and long periods in the air raid shelter in the garden, either waiting for the all-clear or the exploding bombs.

More than 60 years later, Mrs Christine Wright — her married name — recalled:"I can remember having to spend my sister Sylvia's birthday, 16th June 1944, in the air raid shelter and if my memory serves me right, the weather was hot and sunny and all we wanted to do was go outside and play. The air raid shelter was dug underground and topped with grass. We had beds built into either side of the shelter and our parents slept on a mattress on the floor. Unfortunately if the weather was wet, very often the shelter would fill up with water.

"We were very fortunate to have our father with us during the war. He had wanted to join the RAF but was refused as he was an engineer and working on gun turrets for Power Mountings, Tolworth. Many a time Dad came home from work only to have to go out again on fire-watch duty with the Home Guard.

"When the siren sounded my parents would wrap us up in a blanket, take us from our nice warm beds and carry us down to the shelter. Every time I see a beautiful, clear, star-lit sky, it reminds me of those days when I would look up into the sky and see the searchlights penetrating the darkness and watch our planes overhead, obviously going into battle. I was too young then to realise that many of these brave men would never return home to their families.

"We were all made to wear our Micky Mouse gas masks whenever the siren sounded. These were always carried everywhere with you in a box over your shoulder. My baby sister, Maureen, was put into some contraption which looked like a large glass tomb, and which was pumped by hand to supply fresh air to the occupant inside.

"I can also remember men coming round our road and taking down our iron fence and gates. These were collected and taken away to be smelted down and used in the war effort. In the event, most of it was no use.

"In Newlands Way lived the following: No1 — Mr and Mrs Millership, Barbara and Wilfred. They later moved and Mr and Mrs Waites moved in. No 3 — Mrs Watts and her unmarried daughter Elsie. No 5 — Mr and Mrs Pearce, Pamela and John. Pam later emigrated to New Zealand. No 7 — Mr and Mrs Watts, Ralph, Brian, Daphne and Diane. They later emigrated to Rhodesia and unfortunately, Brian died from peritonitis. No 9 — Mr and Mrs Vann, Christine, Sylvia and Maureen. No 11 — Mr and Mrs Sweeney, Michael and Timothy. Michael was later killed in a hit and run tragedy. No 13 was the home of Mr and Mrs Harmes, Terry and Janet and Mrs Henwood, the mother of Mrs Harmes. At No 15 were Mr and Mrs

Newlands Way children gather round a camp fire by a wigwam they put up in a field next to the Clayton Laundry, Clayton Road, Hook, during the Second World War. The meadow was covered in concrete when Woodgate Avenue council estate was built after the war. Left to right are Michael Sweeney, John Pearce, Tim Sweeney, Christine and Maureen Vann, Terry Harmes, Margaret and Brenda Goodway, and Pam Pearce. Terry moved to America. Tim stayed locally, living in Hartfield Road.

Goodway, Brenda and Margaret. Brenda later died from multiple sclerosis.

"Opposite our houses were wide-open spaces and small woods — a children's paradise. It now forms Devon Way. On occasions an old gentleman of the road would make a camp in the trees and we nicknamed him Tarzan. At the back of our houses ran a pathway down to Clayton Road. This went past the Clayton Laundry field, on your right, and if no one was about, we would scrump the apples and pears. Another horrible habit we had was to smoke the pith out of the elderberry bush. Somehow John Pearce always managed to find some matches. The path also led to the Cricketers and often it was my job to fetch Dad a pint of IPA from the pub's off-licence, in a jug.

We were also able to play in the field by the air raid patrol hut — now Woodgate Avenue. In this field was an enormous steam coal dump 'used to keep the steam trains running'. We spent many hours playing on there and getting filthy dirty. We looked for bits of silver paper, dropped

by the Germans intended to interfere with radio signals. As we only lived a short distance from the RAF Hook Balloon Barrage station, this was always being targetted by the Germans. The balloons always reminded me of huge elephants floating in the air, with their big ears.

"We made tents from old bits of material and Dad made kites from pages of the Daily Mirror.

"Most summers, the Romany Gipsies would camp opposite our house. There were two beautifully-kept caravans drawn by horses. I was invited inside and everything was spick and span. The gipsy girl would come and play with us. Her father made pegs and beautiful flowers out of wood which he would whittle at with a knife and then dip into some natural, pinky-coloured dye. Mum always supplied them with water, saying it was an unwritten rule that you always did if the lady gipsy was pregnant."

Marjorie Vann.

Agnes Rundle Muntz, outside the coachman's house, Malvern Lodge, 7 Hook Road, in 1899. The coach-house is still standing but is now incorporated in the Maypole Motors' workshops. It is used as offices for owner, Paul Sparks and the original doorways and windows can still be made out today.

Hetty Muntz was a daughter of Philip Maurice Muntz a yellow metal manufacturer, of Edgbaston, Birmingham, and his wife, Agnes Rundle Muntz, who lived at Malvern Lodge, Hook Road, from 1882 to about 1899. She married William Charles Leader at St Paul's Church, Hook, on September 9th 1893. Earlier, she may have had a friendship with Tolworth landowner Lord Egmont.

The wooded grounds of Malvern Lodge.

A pretty garden path, Malvern Lodge, in 1899.

House in the country opposite The Maypole

Malvern Lodge

ONE of old Hook's most luxurious and largest country houses stood in the peaceful woodland opposite the Maypole public house. The nine-bedroomed mansion was set well back from the main road and was surrounded by sweeping lawns, tennis courts, peach and cucumber houses, and shady glades.

Malvern Lodge, demolished in 1932, after it was sold for a knock-down £2,800, is now remembered in the name of the Malvern Court flats and Malvern Close, built in the grounds soon after its tragic demolition.

Today, the spindly fir trees lining the Hook Road in front of Malvern Court are a living reminder of the past. These trees were planted by a family who lived in the mansion, to mark the boundary with the main road — then a turnpike road for which the fee of a halfpenny had to be paid by travellers to a tollkeeper who lived in Gate House, also demolished and now replaced with the appropriately-named Gate House block of flats on the corner of Ditton Road.

Malvern Lodge appears to have been built in the late 1840s or 1850s but it started its life with the name Lindsay Lodge. It is thought that the original grounds extended to more than seven acres, and took in land where Cotterill Road and Malvern Road were built.

By 1896, the land covered just two and a half acres. It included a

Malvern Lodge (7 Hook Road) standing proud in its heyday.

Driveway to the front of the ivy-covered house.

half-acre meadow opposite today's Midhurst Court, 13 Hook Road.

Lindsay Lodge was so-named by its first inhabitant, Lindsay Wilson, and must have been something to boast about in his classy social circles.

Mr Wilson was still living at the mansion in 1867, but by 1871, new occupants, the Berkeley family, had moved in. Head of the household was Comyns Roland Berkeley, an attorney and solicitor, born in Ongar, Essex. He was 60 years old in 1871, and his Kensington-born wife, Mary, was 45. Their son, Harry, aged 21, followed in his father's footsteps and was an articled clerk to attorney. Younger son, Algernon, aged six, was born in Notting Hill and lived with his family at the country house; his needs attended to by two live-in housemaids.

Tragedy struck in 1880 when another family member, Comyns William Latewaid Berkeley, died aged 32. He is buried at St Paul's churchyard, Hook.

There were few neighbours at the time. Apart from widow, Elizabeth Ludwell, who collected the tolls next door at "Southborough Gate", there were only one or two villas along the Hook (or "Southborough") Road. On the opposite side of the road, a little further up the hill, stood Fairfield (thankfully surviving now as 36 Hook Road). A few plots were being built on next door which were to form St David's Villa, (Holmbury, the Thomas Hardy home now demolished); Devon Villa and Egerton Villa (still standing and now 15 and 17 Hook Road). Hook Villa (Mayfield) and Westfield, forming 19 and 21 Hook Road) are thought to have been completed but were not occupied in 1871. This pair stood on the site of Yew Tree Court.

St Matthew's Church had not then been built, but work was to start within two or three years on the grand place of worship.

Baby Basil Muntz, born in July 1880, at Colwell, Malvern, lived for a time with his grandmother, Eliza Soady, at Egerton Villa, Hook Road. He is pictured here in 1882 at Malvern Lodge with sister, Corrine, born 1869.

Young Basil Muntz. A miniature railway was built in the garden of Malvern Lodge for his pleasure.

Eliza Soady lived at Egerton Villa (Cottage), 17 Hook Road, from 1875 to about 1880. Her daughter, Agnes Rundle Muntz, and son-in-law Philip Maurice Muntz, bought neighbouring Malvern Lodge in 1882.

Midhurst Court, site of St David's Villa — later known as Holmbury — and the pair of semis, Devon Villa and Egerton Villa (later Glenholm) now 13, 15 and 17 Hook Road.

Eliza's husband Robert Williams Soady, a Lincoln's Inn barrister.

Malvern Lodge's residents and family
Upstairs, downstairs life

THE Muntz family moved into Lindsay Lodge, (7 Hook Road), in 1882. The head of the family was Philip Maurice Muntz who owned a yellow metal business in the Midlands with factories at Smethwick and West Bromwich. They quickly changed the name of the country mansion to Malvern Lodge in recognition of the family's former home in the Malvern Hills at Colwell.

Malvern stone was brought to Hook and laid down for tennis courts within the forested gardens set among a small forest.

Philip Maurice Muntz was born in 1841 at Handsworth, Staffs, the son of Philip Henry Muntz, of Handsworth, who died on Christmas Day 1888. Philip junior was 42 years old when he brought his family to Surbiton. The reason is unclear but it was not uncommon for wealthy businessmen to retire early and live the life of a country gent, enjoying sports and other past-times.

Philip's wife was Agnes Rundle Soady, whom he married in 1867. She was about two years younger than him and was brought up in St John's Wood, London.

Agnes and Philip had six children: Corinne, Mabel, Kathleen, Philip, Sybil and Basil. Curiously, Basil, who was born at Colwell, near Malvern, appears to have been partly brought up by his maternal grandmother, Eliza Soady.

Eliza Soady, for reasons not known to her surviving descendents, had come to live in Hook in about 1875, the year Thomas Hardy was in residence at St David's Villa, 13 Hook Road. She moved into Egerton Villa, 17 Hook Road, which was then only two or three years old.

Had she bought the plots and had the small row of villas built? She was widowed in 1857, when her lawyer husband, Robert Williams Soady, of Lincolns Inn, died at the age of 42.

She may have invested any money bequeathed to her in the building plots. The growing town of Surbiton with its relatively new railway station was only a 15-minute walk away.

It is fascinating to discover that Eliza Soady's forefathers, the Brookes family were from Exeter.

To add to the intrigue, however, the first occupant of Devon Villa was Frederick Thuell, whose father was an Exeter man. Frederick was a respected churchwarden of St Paul's Church, Hook. He died aged 47 in March 1876 and is buried in the church's cemetery. A tribute was carried in the parish magazine.

Agnes Rundle Soady, far left, pictured a few years before she moved to Hook from Edgbaston, in the Midlands. In 1867 she married Philip Maurice Muntz (left and below), who ran a yellow metal firm in the Midlands.. Agnes and Philip moved to Malvern Lodge, Hook Road, in 1882, but Agnes's mother, Eliza Soady, had been living at 17 Hook Road since 1876.

A 27ft drawing room and winter garden

On the high road to Hook

MALVERN Lodge went on the market in 1896. The Muntz family, who had been in residence since 1882, decided to move on and instructed the property to be valued. The valuation report has survived intact for more than a century and from this can be gleaned a quite vivid description of the old house and its outbuildings.

It was described as a detached villa residence "on the high road to Hook", containing nine-bedrooms, four dressing rooms, bath room fitted with hot and cold water, WC, a good landing lighted by a skylight, spacious hall, lavatory and WC, dining room 27ft by 15ft exclusive of large bow window, library, drawing room 27ft by 13ft 9" exclusive of a bay window; small conservatory and domestic offices, all on a good scale.

In addition, the grounds contained detached stabling, consisting of two loose boxes, two stalls, harness room, two good double coach houses, loft and two living rooms. There was a paved yard and folding gates to the High Road (Hook Road); potting sheds, an exclusive range of span roof glass houses consisting of stove house, two greenhouses and two vineries and a cucumber house and orchid house all heated by one boiler.

There were also two peach houses, together 77ft, heated by a separate boiler.

The five-and-a-half-acre grounds were arranged as a flower garden with ashphalt and a lawn tennis court. There was a kitchen garden, orchard and an extensive plantation, chiefly of Scotch firs.

On the north side of the plantation, there was a frontage of about 180ft, known as Cotterill Road, which was "not apparently taken over by the local authorities" and this road formed part of a building estate which had affected the enjoyment of the occupants of Malvern Lodge.

The valuator pointed out that Malvern Lodge had been added to in degrees and "was not very satisfactory", especially the reception rooms.

Furthermore, he was not impressed with the grounds, saying they "do not possess any special beauty" and "do not justify the place fetching any fancy price."

He concluded that there was an element of value in the property as a building estate, assuming an outlet can be obtained in the Cottrell Road as, from the shape of the estate, a road could with little or no waste of land, be run through from the main road. There was also a note to say the grounds included the meadow on the opposite side of the "High Road" of about 182ft which is "valuable for building". The whole estate was valued at £7,100.

The departure of the Muntz family marked the end of an era. The family was regarded as notable gentry. The servants wore a livery of dark green. Philip Maurice Muntz was the grandson of Philip Frederick Muntz, who came to England from the continent in 1783 and settled

The drawing room, Malvern Lodge, in 1931. A door led into a winter garden with goldfish pond.

at Selly Wick, Worcestershire. Philip Maurice Muntz's father, Philip Henry Muntz, of Edstone Hall, Warwickshire, was a JP and MP for Birmingham, 1865-1885 and twice mayor of Birmingham.

Philip Maurice Muntz died on 9th January 1899, less than three years after leaving Hook.

His grandson, John Last, of Whitchurch, Shropshire, has maintained an interest in his forefathers' Hook days and in the year 2001, his mother, the daughter, of Hetty Muntz, was still alive and well, and in her eighties.

He has told how his grandmother, Hetty Muntz, used to go into the long hot-houses early and select peaches before the gardener could interfere. His grandmother also spoke of an archery ground in the gardens.

Some years after his death, Philip Maurice Muntz's widow, Agnes, moved to her ancestors' home town of Exeter and is listed at two addresses at St David's Hill in the city, lending weight to a possible theory that she was involved in some way in the Hook Road properties of St David's Villa - Thomas Hardy's home in 1874-5 - Devon Villa, and maybe Devonshire Villas in Ditton Road.

The Muntz family's home county, however, was Warwickshire and there were strong links with Rugby. Perhaps that is how the family of Reverend George Chatterton Richards had such a long link with St

David's Villa, for the clergyman came from Rugby and he attended Rugby School and became known in the high society circles through his friendship with respected college masters there. Sir Philip Albert Muntz was a governor of Rugby School.

After the Muntz family moved away, a family named Pinnock moved into Malvern Lodge. They were tenants of Mr E Bloomfield, the owner. Thereafter the Popkiss family were in residence until 1931.

In 1978, Barclay Popkiss recalled: "My father (Richard) bought Malvern Lodge in 1912. I believe it had been vacant for some time. There were about two-and-a-half acres of land with many beautiful trees — a feature being the chestnuts, in particular one at the end of the lawn.

"There had been considerably more land at one time, but part had been sold off and Malvern Road was constructed at the back — on our boundary — this land had been developed, as I remember when we lived at Malvern Lodge and houses had been built on it to some depth.

"Owing to age and ill-health and expense of upkeep, my father decided to sell in 1931. However, it did not sell, probably owing to the slump and was withdrawn. My father died in 1932 and for various reasons it became imperative that I should sell as one of his executors. A salesman negotiated in January 1933 at a very bad time and at a knockdown price of £2,800! A builder from New Malden knocked the house down."

Vane Cottage

The roof of Hook's oldest surviving house, Vane Cottage (c1669) was damaged after the first doodlebug in the borough of Surbiton fell on nearby Whitehall Crescent on 17th June 1944.

For more than 50 years, from 1890 or earlier, the Poultons and their descendents lived at Vane Cottage, 435 Hook Road. Here, in the 1940s, are some of them: Top: Shirley, Betty, Posy, Duggie and Mary. Bottom row: Reggie, Emily, Millie, Ernie, Johnny, and Joan.

Arcade Parade, Elm Road

HK.7 HOOK.

Copyright T. Sergean

Elm Road and Arcade Parade, Hook, in 1951, four years before the Crown Post Office was built at the end of the parade. The garden containing the horse chestnut tree, then part of Rhodrons land was bought for the development. The post office front counter was closed in about 1989. In the 1990s the building was used as offices for the Chessington Hook and Malden Rushett Neighbourhood Committee. The furthest shop seen is Vogue ladies' hair stylists. The cars are parked outside L.E.Webb's chemist and the gas show-rooms. A Ganley's fruiterers is on the far right of the picture. Many of the old cottages in Elm Road are still standing and have taken on a pretty, rustic appearance. Just out of view is A.C.Benn's newsagents at 379 Hook Road. Arthur Benn's son, Jeff, a keen ornithologist now living in Devon, helped to run the branch while Duncan and Mavis Miller managed another branch at 316 Hook Road in the 1960s and 1970s.

Sent from New Zealand: A previously unknown photo of Whitehall, which stood on the site of Whitehall Crescent from the 1830s to 1938.

Croquet on the lawn at Whitehall (The Manor House)

WHITEHALL was a nine-bedroom mansion with a coach house and gardener's cottage. It stood from the 1830s or earlier until 1938 when it was demolished and Whitehall Crescent was built. From 1839-41, the first minister of St Paul's Church, Hook, Rev John McGammon Trew, lived there. By 1871, William Wareham, born in London in 1823, and his wife, Mary Ann, (*pictured right*) were in residence and stayed into the 1880s. He drowned in a maritime disaster off Ilfracombe, in 1887. He and Mary Ann had 11 children. Three daughters are seen here playing croquet on the lawn. A son, George, (*pictured left*) and his wife, emigrated to New Zealand in 1882. George's grand-daughter Elaine, aged 80 in 2001, supplied these remarkable pictures.

Drowned: William Wareham, in earlier years with his wife, Mary, and their three daughters, Mary, Margaret and Emily. The family lived at Whitehall, Hook, from the late 1870s to the late 1880s. Tragedy struck in 1887 when Mr Wareham drowned at sea.

Tragic death of father

TRAGEDY hit a Hook family in August 1887 while they were on a summer holiday in Devon. William Wareham, a Kingston JP, of The Manor House (also known as Whitehall) Hook, was staying in Ilfracombe and had boarded with 23 others the 10-ton pleasure yacht, Monarch.

The sea was calm but a sudden gust of wind caused the boat to reel and a hook slid off the deck into the water. The captain decided to turn back to fetch it and a fierce squall caught the sails. The boat took on water and capsized. All but four of the 24 passengers were submerged. Fourteen were rescued but 14 lost their lives in the horrendous accident.

Elaine Barron, the great grand-daughter of William Wareham on a visit from New Zealand to England in 2000.

Condemned cottages on the crest of a hill
'The Aged Dame' at Hook

THANKS to the diaries kept from 1890-1892 by a Surbiton shopkeeper and artist, a fascinating insight can be obtained of a Hook grocery shop. William Freeman and his wife used to take frequent walks into the countryside of Hook and Chessington in that late Victorian era. And on hot summer days, they cherished a refreshment stop in Hook Road (then called Leatherhead Road south of the North Star) at a little shop at the end of a row of about nine terraced cottages.

These run-down cottages were nearing the end of their life and in 1892 were soon to be pulled down to be replaced with four detached Victorian villas, now 254, 256, 258, and 260 Hook Road (see picture opposite). A graphic description of this terrace and the shop, run by an old woman and her son, is provided by William Freeman's diary and sketch pad. He called there on 12th June 1892 and put pen to paper and drew the above illustration.

He wrote: "When you come to the western end of our road *(Victoria Road, Surbiton)* and turn right angles and heading south, you are in the Hook Road. On to Hook is rather up and down through a nice open country. The third crest has a row of very low cottages of one storey. They have been whitewashed and possibly years ago were considered very desirable premises. At the least dilapidated, goods are sold for the benefit of the other cottages — bacon, tobacco, sugar and sweet stuff, with the usual candles and ginger beer.

"We had been at Surbiton a little while before we first stopped at this cottage shop. It must have been in the summer of 1880. Then, the terrace was still let. My aged dame seemed quite an old woman when we first saw her, but active enough for her little business.

"Sometimes our ginger beer was given us by a big man, her son, and

The Aged Dame at her Hook grocery, in 1892.

very occasionally by a thin-faced woman, presumably the son's wife. We have stopped in our walk scores of times on the crest of the hill and refreshed ourselves at this place.

"But now all the other cottages are empty and most of the windows are broken or out. This is through our refined sanitary management. The cottages have been condemned by the local authority, all but the dame's. They were let for 3/6 weekly, while the shop at the end, being a double one and having a good piece of ground, pays 8/-. This 8/- a week with a supplementary 5/- weekly, is the total income of the owner of the estate, another aged dame *(believed to be Christiana Hansell)*.

"The owner, not having capital to effect the required improvements, has lost most of her income. The selling price she asked for the property when the cottages were let was £1,500. She was offered £1,200. Now she asks £900 and won't take £700.

"My survivor was 82 last week. Her son is about 55. The old lady is very cheerful and makes light of her infirmaries. A short while ago she was bedridden, but has come out again, and last Wednesday evening, returning from a walk, I called in and had the ginger beer as of yore.

She was sitting behind the rough deal counter and greeted me pleasantly. The aged one admitted that she couldn't do much now. Upon my query: 'Aren't you over eighty?', she told me the year of her birth and what she could remember. 'Waterloo? Oh yes. And the old king dying. And Napoleon's death.'

She was at work in the fields at George III's death *(1820)*, so she has worked for more or less 70 years. Now it is nearly over, though I asked her to live for another reign and make it five. She laughed but seemed doubtful."

❏ *The Aged Dame, although not named in Mr Freeman's diary, is almost certainly Sophia Marchant, born 1809 in East Grinstead. She had an unmarried son, Thomas, born c1838, in Balcombe, and a washerwoman daughter, Maria, a spinster, born in 1851 at Wakefield, Sussex.*

"An ineligible investment at Hook" — the terrace demolished in the 1890s. Sketches by William Freeman, 1892.

Ella and William Joseph Maywood, born 1859 and 1860, lived for many years in one of the four detached late Victorian villas in the Hook Road, a few yards from what is now the petrol station on the corner of Somerset Avenue. Their house was called Burleigh — now No 258. It is the second house from the left in the picture. Mr Maywood was a headmaster at a Kingston school and a controversial churchwarden at Hook. The little girl, Betty Smith (no connection with a late resident of a nearby bungalow) pictured right is the Maywoods' grand-daughter. Her mother Margaret Octavia was the eighth child of the Maywoods. The youngster is seen playing happily in the front garden of Burleigh in about 1921. The first of the villas, now No 260, was known as Rosslyn, and from 1950 for at least 50 years, was home to Mrs Betty Rhodes. No 256 was called Carmarthen and in the 1920s was the residence of Fred and Mary Williams. At No 254 (Northfield) lived 65 bus conductoress Maureen Notton.

Some bygone shops

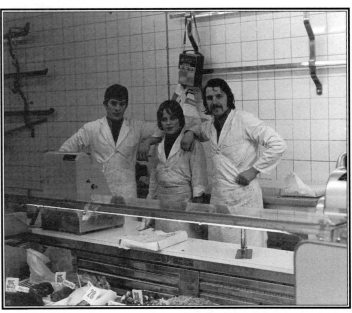

Matthews, the butchers, traded during the 1950s, 1960s and 1970s near the corner of Hook Road and Clayton Road. In the 1990s, the premises became a fish and chip takeaway, Mr Chips.

Oakey's stores, 140 Hook Road, in about 1960.

Shoppers make their selections at the counter of J.S.Sainsbury's store, Ace Parade, Hook, in the mid 1970s. The branch was to close in 1980 after a larger Sainsbury's opened in Surbiton and is now The Regent Chinese restaurant. Singer Cliff Richard has been seen dining here. During the Second World War, an Ack Ack gun was positioned on the roof above the staff and a soldier could be seen training binoculars on the surrounding landscape from his elevated viewpoint. It is said the weighty gun caused damage to the roof.

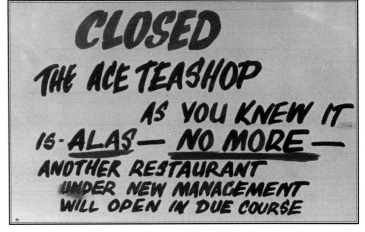

CLOSED
THE ACE TEASHOP
AS YOU KNEW IT
IS - ALAS — NO MORE —
ANOTHER RESTAURANT
UNDER NEW MANAGEMENT
WILL OPEN IN DUE COURSE

Off the boil: The Ace Teashop shut in October 1976.

St Paul's head, Arthur Harrold, seated, at his farewell in 1946. Staff include Fred Clark, top left, Joan Rumble and Ethel Rook, third and second from top right.

Lessons 1908 style at Hook School, Orchard Road. Among the pupils is Edith Parsons, born 1902 at 37 Thornhill Road, daughter of Joseph.

Children of St Paul's School, Hook, and some of their parents gather in October 1969 in the school hall to bid farewell to teacher Fred Clark after 32 years of devoted service.

All but four of a class of 31 children at St Paul's School in the 1960s attended a happy reunion of ex-pupils in 1995. Retired headmaster Stan Lacey took a mock assembly — with a hymn — at the school.

The old Hook Vicarage – open fires, summer fairs and rats

A fete at the old Hook Vicarage in about 1955. The photo was sent to David Tippett-Wilson by Rev John Balcom, of Massachusetts, who spent a year at Hook in an exchange with St Paul's vicar, Rev. Selwyn Taborn. Mr Balcom found the building cold and draughty. Open fires had to be lit for warmth and he saw rats. The building and its very long garden were sold in 1959. A new vicarage was later built opposite. Petula Clark once sang at a fete in the old Vicarage, now vanished.

HK.15 Surbiton Road, HOOK.

Copyright
T. Sergeant

Nash's Maythorne Laundry (right) closed more than 30 years ago after trading since 1935, although there had been a laundry on the site since Edwardian times, run then by Frank Searle. The building and the attached house appear to have been constructed on the site of an earlier dwelling called Seabreeze Cottage. The laundry was taken over in 1935 by Robert Kenrick Nash, whose family had owned laundries at Kennington, Brixton, Eastbourne and Brighton. The laundry is recalled in the name of a cottage at 61 Thornhill Road. Doreen Conroy gave her home this name because her mother, Lilian Wells, was a former ironer at the laundry. Lilian had got the job after fleeing from an undesirable position as a maid in a big old house in Maple Road, Surbiton in 1918. In 2001, the old house and laundry buildings were still standing but had been greatly altered at the front, forming the Hewden Tool and Equipment Hire Centre. In this early 1950s postcard, the caption writer has been confused by the road name.

Familiar faces

Henry 'Harry' Ash was a familiar face in the Ace of Spades area. He lived in Kent Way but in 1991, he died aged 85 in a road accident near the Lucky Rover, Hook Road. This fine portrait was taken by Fred Wilgoss, owner of the DIY shop on the corner of Hook and Haycroft Roads for many years.

The death occurred in 1999 of Miss Joan Rumble, at the age of 85. She taught at St Paul's, 1940-1972.

Authoress and journalist Gwendolen Freeman of 416 Hook Road, Hook, pictured in April 2000. She spent her girlhood at Shirley, 62 Hook Road.

Mary and Michael Creane clocked up 20 years running the Lucky Rover in 2001.

The staff of St Paul's School, Hook, c1976, with Roger Finch, headmaster from 1976 to July 2001.

Dennis Stickley — forefathers came from Dorset and farmed Hook.

Peter Muggleton, resident of 10 Kelvin Grove for 35 years and a popular patron of the Lucky Rover.

Betty Smith lived at Cyron, 266 Hook Road, from 1925 until her death in 1999. She was a keen bird lover.

'Robbie" Robertson, who lived at 272 Hook Road, was organist at St Paul's, Hook, close to his home.

Philip Menhennet in 1998. He was scout leader and group leader of 1st Hook in the 1950s and 1960s and in the year 2000 could still be seen at scout fairs.

World-famous airman Harry Hawker lived at Ennadale, Hook Road, next to the junction with Orchard Road. He died aged 32 when his plane crashed. He is buried in St Paul's Church, Hook.

Old boots in a well
Shoemaker

Olds boots: Henry Butler.

HENRY Butler, a shoemaker from Peterborough, moved to Clyde Cottage, Clayton Road, in 1880. In 1991, divers probed the old village well opposite and discovered many old boots.

Jeanne and her parents, Evelyn and James Chappell.

ST PAUL'S Church, Hook, was full to capacity for the funeral service held after the death on 24th August 1999, of its much-respected verger, Jeanne Moore, of 120 Clayton Road. She was 75. Jeanne had given much of her life to the church, as had her mother, Evelyn, before her. Jeanne had served as verger for 40 years.

The Ace of Spades roundabout in the 1950s when the underpass was still just a plan on a drawing board.

THE Ace of Spades roundabout a few years before the construction in 1959 of the Hook Underpass. The News of the World advertisement is outside Seymour's newsagent's shop which became Woodward's. In 1918, to confuse the postman, this was numbered 5 Hook Road, but no 7 was Malvern Lodge, half a mile away near The Maypole. Around the time of the First World War, The Southborough Stores traded next door to Seymour's. The next shop along was run by Emma and Maurice Brooker, whose premises were then called Bradford House. Walter Aggas ran the boot and shoe shop next door to the Brookers. The Aggas home was called Northampton House — an indication, perhaps, of the strong association of Northampton with shoes. The Southborough Arms was the next premises along, next to Haycroft Road, some of whose cottages can be seen in the photo to the rear of the new Southborough Arms, constructed in the early 1930s.

On New Year's Eve, 1936, there was a "gay cabaret" at the Ace of Spades Restaurant, featuring comedian Arthur Askey who "cracked topical jokes and sang amusingly". The joyous evening also included the Andalusian Trio — "three girls who danced in the rhythmic Spanish style".

Building of the Hook Underpass, 1959.

Vale Road evacuated

Hook Road after the great storm of Friday July 6th 1973.

Vale Road South – later condemned

Sydney de Carle started the hairdresser's at 75 Hook Road in 1932. His son, Michael, (above) took over in 1959 and in 2001 celebrated his 70th birthday.

CLASS differences a century ago were much more pronounced than they are today. Even after the First World War, children from the villas along Hook Road were forbidden from playing with the poor people's youngsters from the Vale Road Victorian terraces.

One mother told her daughter: "Don't go down Vale Road. There's fever there."

Vale Road South's 19 terraced cottages were built in about 1881 and provided affordable homes for young families not just from Hook but further afield, too. George Simmonds, a stoker, and his wife, and 14-year-old son, Walter, a telegraph boy, were the first occupants of No 1. They hailed from Great Bookham. George Isdderson, a general labourer and his wife, Ellen and their six children, squeezed into No 2 in 1881. Thomas Wright, a house painter, lived at No 7. His baby daughter, Kate, was born at the cottage.

Some ninety years later, in 1973, a thunderstorm of tropical intensity sounded the eventual death knell for the terrace in Vale Road South. In the monsoon conditions of Friday afternoon, 6th July 1973, 4.65ins of rain fell in about 90 minutes. Only one other storm in the whole of Greater London had ever been heavier.

The little brook by Vale Road North turned into a raging river, the likes of which had never been seen. Water several feet deep surged into the Vale properties trapping people in upstairs rooms.

Bob Sewell, of Hook Evangelical Church, and other members of the congregation clubbed together to effect a rescue. Boats were launched to reach the stricken. One disaster followed another that night. Bob put up a ladder to Nellie Green's home. She said she wouldn't come out because she didn't have any clean smalls and they were on the line. He went on to rescue a child from another house but the mother appeared hysterical and accidentally kicked the ladder. Bob fell off and ended up in hospital. Luckily he only suffered bruising.

The terrace took months to dry out and during the rehousing, squatters and drug addicts moved in. Some died there. Eventually the cottages were condemned and pulled down.

Court Crescent celebrates

THE war has come to an end and it's time to celebrate the end of the hostilities and allow life to slowly get back to normal. These two pictures show the residents of Court Crescent, off Mansfield Road, rejoicing. The picture below was taken in a hall at Chessington.

Court Crescent takes it name from Chessington Court Farm, which stood opposite the White Hart, Hook, until its demolition in 1952 when it was replaced by the Holmwood Road, Shere, Albury and Frimley Close development. In Leatherhead Road, Chessington, close to Chessington Parade shops, there is still a small terrace of of old houses, called Court Cottages, which were used to house the agricultural labourers working for the Moon family which kept Chessington Court Farm.

Court Crescent was built in the early 1930s and about a dozen of the Ransom-built homes were allocated for carpenters working for Betty Joel Ltd, furniture manufacturers, Hook Rise North, in premises which became Gala cosmetics. Lord Mountbatten was among the firm's clients.

The company paid £25 deposit on each of the houses as an incentive to encourage carpenters to move to the area from Portsmouth. Among those who did relocate was the father of Vi Goldsack, who moved into No 6 in 1930 as a teenager and stayed until 1950 before moving with her husband to, Ray, to 40 Cox Lane. In August 2001, Mrs Goldsack was still living at the house. Her husband died 16 years previously. Mrs Goldsack had worked at a plastics factory off Hook Rise, cutting up printed staff identity cards.

Top: Court Crescent residents celebrate VJ day in 1945. The furthest left in the bottom row of standing adults is Mrs Stripp, landlady of the White Hart. Her daughter, Norah, is by her side. A long-time resident of the crescent, Mrs Boatright, is in the same row. The sitting girl first on the left is Winnie Marsden. In the second row from the top, fifth from right, is Violet Goldsack.

Right: Court Crescent families at an end-of-war tea party held at a Chessington hall. In the bottom row, on the extreme left, is a Mrs Williams and next to her are Mr and Mrs Rosewell.

The Loggia dining area at the Ace of Spades. Inset: Boxer Max Baer.

The Dance Room: War hero pilot Douglas Bader was a patron.

Mock Tudor: the Ace of Spades.

Cosy corners for romantic chats.

The Sun Lounge at the Ace of Spades Road House, Hook, in its hey day.

Ace of Spades Road House, Hook

Ace of Spades Road House, Kingston By-Pass.

The Ace of Spades Roadhouse was a most popular venue soon after the Kingston by-pass was opened in the late 1920s. The mock Tudor nightclub, dance hall, restaurant, tearooms and open air swimming pool drew clientele from a wide area. It was fashionable to motor to Hook on the new road from far-flung parts of London to enjoy the all-night facilities. Boxer Max Baer trained here.

More than a century of worship

Hook Evangelical Church

FOR more than a century the message of the gospel has been preached in Brook Road, Hook. Little is known about the early years of the 'Hook Mission' but the first church building in the road, then called St James Road, Southborough, was said to be in 1878.

The little church would have served as a place of worship for the farming families in the village and perhaps some of the servants and maids working in the Victorian villas along the Hook Road.

In 1900, St James Road was renamed Brook Road and four years later, the church was officially registered for religious worship.

In Edwardian times, the church was linked with the Pentecostals, the Baptists and the Anglicans. In particular, Oaklands Baptist Church, Surbiton Hill, was responsible for supplying speakers for Sunday services. In 1905 a Mr B Medcalf, corn merchant, owned the building.

In February 1905, the small congregation were shocked at the "painfully sudden death" of Rev Walter Henry Powell, pastor of the mission, at the time called "Hook Baptist Church". His death occurred at his residence, 1 North View, Brook Road, soon after he had returned home from a Band of Hope meeting and while sitting in a chair, he was "seized with illness and expired shortly afterwards." Dr Mowll, of Hook Road, formed the opinion he had died from a haemorrhage.

Mr Powell, who was 59, had come to Hook in November 1903 and the following month "opened the mission in Brook Road", of which he undertook the superintendency.

"After the mission had been in existence some time it was thought it would be wise to form it into a church and in June 1904, the charge of the church was delivered to the deceased by Rev L O Stalberg of Kingston," reported the Surrey Comet. "A Sunday School, Band of Hope and other organisations were also formed and at the present day they are flourishing branches of the church."

The newspaper wrote that Mr Powell was an earnest worker and was well-known in other places where, prior to coming to Hook, he had been actively engaged in evangelical work." He is buried in Hook Churchyard at St Paul's Church.

During these early years, Charles Walter, a Christian solicitor, of Surbiton Hill, bought the church premises for about £600 and supplied a pastor, A.J. Phillips, who had been working locally for two years as a colporteur. The church went from strength to strength. To safeguard its future, the premises' freehold was transferred to the Evangelisation Society.

In 1914, the good works were undone by the outbreak of the First World War and only a handful of people were left to attend services. The Evangelisation Society sent the Henman brothers to Hook and they looked after the spiritual welfare of the neighbourhood for periods during and after the war. Mr G.W. Skipper also provided valuable help.

Unwelcome news came in 1922 when Surbiton Council ordered

Hook Mission Church, Brook Road. The date on the masonry of the original building appears to read 1881, or 1891, under which are the words 'Mission Hall'.

Bill and Gillian Aldred, of 12 Herne Road, had served Hook Evangelical Church for many years when this photograph was taken in 2001. Gillian attended the church as a child.

structural repairs to the church. The growing congregation also needed more space. A rebuilding programme was drawn up and a fund launched. In 1928, a classroom, kitchen and vestry were added. Around this time, the Stickley family farmers provided haycarts to take children on Sunday outings to Box Hill.

In 1941, the church was licensed to hold weddings. Satellite Sunday schools were held at Mansfield Road estate and at Moor Lane School. This led to the building of Chessington Evangelical Church in 1958 at Bridge Road.

Dennis Fox became superintendent in 1950 and served for six years and then Harold Sayer took over. Will Morrow was in charge from 1960-4.

By the late 1950s, plans were made to rebuild the old church. A new building, including a small hut, kitchen and vestry, was dedicated on 17th March 1962. Three years later the church appointed its first full-time pastor after a succession of honorary superintendents. Rev Brian Edwards took over the new post in January 1966 and remained in the position until the late 1995.

The classrooms at the rear of the church were rebuilt in 1974, resulting in the large hall and other rooms used today. In 1977, an outreach Sunday School was started on the Sunray estate.

Expansion again posed a happy problem in 1981 and the congregation considered the options, voting overwhelmingly to rebuild at Brook Road rather than relocate. At least £113,000 was needed and many prayers were answered when £10,000 was offered in the first month and £40,000 promised. There was even an anonymous donation of £25,000. By November 1982, the major revamp had been completed and the builders' bills settled. Rev Paul Pease took over in 1997.

The old Maypole, 2 Hook Road, before its replacement in 1904. A tollgate was sited here until 1883. Ditton Road is on the right.

Maypole and the tollgate

THE old, humble, Maypole public house was replaced by a newer hostelry in 1904. Behind the former building can be seen the chimney pots of some older cottages — thought to be Southborough Dairy, no longer standing. The Swift family lived in Middlecot, two doors up at No 6 (later No 10). Phoebe Swift was a remembered by a former neighbour as being a "nice woman with pale, brown hair and blue eyes" who taught at Tiffins Girls, Penrhyn Road, Kingston. Some pupils would deliberately annoy her. One girl would wedge a knitting needle under her desk lid and keep pinging it. Pupil Gwendolen Freeman, from Hook Road, recalled making a contoured map of Africa which turned out to look "like a rabbit's insides." The gentle Miss Swift commented: "Oh well, you've done your best."

Miss Swift's white-haired cousin, Miss Jessie Hare, also lived at the house, still standing and once owned by snooker player Jimmy White.

Now the Maypole's next-door neighbour is No 8 — in the year 2001, the surgery of Scotsman Dr Mackie. The row of houses, Nos 8 to 20 Hook Road were built in about 1902-4. Opposite the Maypole was the former Southborough tollgate keeper's home, and next door a chemist's from the 1920s to the 1940s run by Richard and Louisa Evans. Outside was a grotesque wooden statue of a man or creature with a face like a gargoyle.

Gate House, 1 Hook Road, (right) was pulled down about 1960 and replaced by flats of the same name. In the 1920s, the Gaze family, builders, lived at the old house. There were four daughters.

Long history of a thriving troop

1st Hook Scouts

THE 1st Hook Scouts has seen thousands of boys pass through the organisation since its official foundation in 1923 and it is still a thriving group today.

It is possible the cubs scouts section had been holding meetings unofficially as early as 1909.

The group's first leader was Dickie Cole. In 1924, a rover crew for young men aged between 18 and 25 was started up under the leadership of Alf Ashborne and the first of many rover dinners was held on 5th November.

In 1934, Harold Oakey became scout master and was quickly christened Skipper. There were then only 12 boys in the troop but by the next year the number had risen to 27 and the scouts won the Tipkee flag and cup. The growing membership meant a permanent meeting place was needed and a fundraising campaign was launched.

In 1937, a group committee was founded and a display staged. Plans were drawn up for a headquarters 60ft long and 25ft wide.

The following year, the band was founded. For 1/6d (8p) an hour, a local Territorial Army member provided two hours' training a week. The land set aside for the headquarters — on what is now the rear of Verona Drive and Kent Way — was purchased for £178.

The outbreak of war in 1939 meant plans for the headquarters were put on hold and the land was let out for allotments. Anti-gas measures were explained at weekly meetings once they resumed. The group set about collecting waste paper to help the war effort as well as raise funds for the new headquarters. In 1940 'Skipper' Oakey was called up for service and 'Gaffer' Horton took over as scout master. Tents had to be camouflaged.

World War Two shelters at Hook Recreation Ground.

Founding members of the 1st Hook Scouts in about 1923. In the bottom row, seated, first from the left is George Winstone, of Cissendune, 237 Hook Road. Second from the left is a lad called Ashborne, whose family ran a carpet and furnishings shop at Ewell Road, Tolworth. The top row includes (first from the left) 'Fatty' Sims, whose family owned the brickfields at Claygate; second left, Bill Winstone, third from left, Harold Oakey and sixth from the left Roly Newman, who became an engineer with National Cash Registers.

The regular venue, Hook and Southborough Parish Hall, opened in 1926, was turned into a British Restaurant and scout meetings were moved to Tolworth Central Hall, now Tolworth Girls' School.

An air scout troop was formed in 1941 by Wilf Sayer, of Hillview, Hook Road. In 1943, the founder, Dickie Cole, died.

In 1944, a good number of boys were evacuated out of the area when doodlebug raids started and troop meetings were depleted of members. Skipper Oakey returned from war service in 1945 and took over the reigns from 'Gaffer' Horton. The rover crew was re-formed under the leadership of Ralph Oakey.

With the war out of the way, a camp was held in the long, hot summer of 1947 at Milford on Sea where trapped rabbits went some way to eke out the meat rations. Meetings returned to the parish hall the following year and the band was re-formed.

In 1948, meetings were once again held in the parish hall and a senior troop was formed. In 1949 Jack Wilson and Harry Chatfield took the senior scouts on a camp to Jersey. The following year work started on building the Verona Drive HQ. It was opened on 22nd September 1951 and a grand fete was held to mark the occasion. A guild of old scouts was formed to help pals keep in touch.

In 1953, the year of the Queen's Coronation, the group became an 'open' one, having previously been tied to St Paul's Church.

In 1954, the first scouters' dinner was held in the HQ and the next year, Philip Menhennet took over as scoutmaster, leaving 'Skipper' Oakey as group scout master. Two years later, Eileen Wilson, nee Newark, stood down as leader of A-pack cubs and Roy Dack took over.

The year 1959 saw Skipper Oakey clock up 25 years' service to 1st Hook. In 1960, Colin Smith re-formed the rover crew.

During 1961 an ex-army hut from Richmond Park was purchased. It was erected at the rear of the HQ to provide a new rover and guild den. Three years later, Skipper Oakey officially retired and Phil Menhennet took over the role as group scoutmaster. In 1967 the band won three trophies in a national scout band contest. The summer fete was revived and the A-pack cubs triumphed at a swimming gala.

Colin Smith died in 1969 but his inspiration lived on. In 1973, the group celebrated its 50th anniversary with a camp at Walton Firs. a church parade and dinner at Surbiton Assembly Rooms.

Phil Menhennet retired the next year and was succeeded by Tony Edwards. Ralph Oakey's death was mourned the same year. Work started on a £45,000 project to rebuild the HQ. It was ready by 1975. In 1977, Lord Baden Powell, grandson of the founder attended a display.

In 1978, the band played in the Lord Mayor's show and the first girls joined the ventures. A minibus was bought to help with transport. The following year the group purchased its first coach and a van and some months later, Mr Menhennet was appointed county commissioner. The troop mourned the death at an early age of Ann Thorne, a former cub leader with B-pack.

In 1984, after some action-packed years, Tony Edwards retired as group scout leader; his place was taken by Neil Winckless. Plans were drawn up for another stage of the HQ extension.

The year 1985 saw the Navaho beaver colony formed and Tony Edwards appointed district commissioner for Kingston and Malden District. David Carrick took over from David Deane as scout leader.

Bob Bushell was appointed district commissioner for Surbiton District in 1986 and the same year David Thompson took over the band from Richard Hackett. Three familiar faces over the years, Mike Howe, Doug New and Bill Richardson passed away.

In 1987, Harold Oakey celebrated his 80th birthday. The band achieved a national status grade A at its annual inspection. Group stalwart George Winstone, of 233 Hook Road, died.

Golden jubilee celebrations were held by the band in 1988 and they performed as a guest band at the Royal Tournament. The scout coach and lorry had their gear boxes stolen at the same time from the HQ. The coach had to be scrapped.

The roof of the HQ was replaced at a cost of £7,700.

In 1990, the group visited Denmark, where many long-standing friendships had been made within the scouting fraternity over the years. In 1991 girls were admitted to all sections of the group and the 1st Hook went from strength to strength in the next decade.

1st Hook Scouts march down Hook Road past Moore's Bakery, at the junction of Somerset Avenue, Hook, on Sunday 6th July 1941.

A 1st Hook reunion and get-together for the group's golden jubilee celebrations in 1973.

Ace of Spades pool, 1941

The winner of the junior swimming championship is congratulated by the opponents at the side of the Ace of Spades pool in the gala of 1941. The event was organised by Wilf Sayer, of Hook Road.

Winners: Top, left to right, T. Laidler, B. Evans, I. Green, T. Ambrose, and J. Cram. Seated, K. Powell, E. Maydon, D. May, A Harris and Speakman.

An inter scout troop swimming gala was held at the Ace of Spades pool, Hook Rise North, on Sunday 31st August 1941. The pool was part of the Ace of Spades roadhouse and was a major attraction for partygoers and night-time visitors who sat at the pool-edge with their drinks, or took part in high-spirited larking around involving people falling in. On one occasion the pool owner was in trouble with the local council when the water leaked on to the Kingston by-pass. She refused to drain the pool and repair it so the Fire Brigade arrived uninvited, along with the national press and forced its emptying. Some years later the pool sadly disappeared under an enlarged A3 dual carriageway. Here it is in its heyday.

Family in the hut

VICTORIAN Hook was vastly different from today's bustling suburbia. In Hook Road, opposite Haycroft Road, were a couple of ramshackle old cottages dotted around a large field and smallholdings approached only by a long path next to an orchard.

Joseph and Lillian Parsons and some of their eight or more children lived in 1900 at a property called simply 'the hut' before moving in 1902 to No 37 Thornhill Road. The hut's precise location is in some doubt but descendants of the family were told the 'bungalow' was next to a piggery to the rear of the Maythorne Laundry and Stickley's yard (now 171 Hook Road and used by Surbiton Tyres).

A voters' list for 1901 records Joseph Parsons as living at 'the hut', Hook Road, but by 1906 a similar list refers only to a Herbert Parsons living in the same locality at a property called The Arbour; this name meaning a place hidden by tree branches. Herbert was probably Joseph's son by his first marriage.

A little further down Hook Road, where Verona Drive has been built, in the former Southborough Brickworks field was a very old country cottage in the shape of an ornamental cheese dish. Before numbering, it was known as Field Cottage. In the 1920s, the Eede family lived there. Walter Thomas Eede, a Sussex-born man, worked for farmer Moon, of Chessington Court Farm, opposite the White Hart, Hook. The Arbour and Field Cottage may well be different names for the same dwelling. The Arbour was also known as The Harbour or, unofficially, even Harbour Lights.

Miss Farmer, of Ewell Road, would call for the rent, walking over the field in a dignified manner, holding up a parasol.

There was a cesspit down the bottom of the garden, no electricity or gas in the 1940s and illumination came from candles or "a little old oil lamp." Round the back of the house was where the cows were kept. The cattle belonged to William B Farmer, of Ewell Road and there were a good number of steers.

Walter Eede's grandson, Bob Sewell, born in 1935, moved from Southampton to Field Cottage as a young child. His aunt and uncle, Victor and Nellie Eede, also lived at the cottage, along with Bob's parents, Violet and Bob snr. Young Bob became a pupil at Hook School in Orchard Road. He recalls

Field Cottage, also known as Harbour Lights, in 1930. See also p3.

The Parsons family who lived in a hut: Bessie, Joseph, Fran, Monte, Lill, Lillian, Flo and Maude.

YOUNG Charlie Parsons, known as Monte, was a mischievous child. He sometimes went alone into the farm field behind the allotments and rode a horse bare-back. If found he would be reprimanded, ending up not only with sore thighs from riding, but also with a sore rear from the punishment.

Many years later, Monte had his love of horses fulfilled when he joined a horse regiment in the Great War. When the war ended he returned to the family home, then in Douglas Road, Tolworth. The news of his return from the battlefields reached a delighted nephew, Carl Bryant, also living at the house. Carl was at the time washing in a tin bath but leapt out naked and ran down the road to greet his uncle. Granny Parsons went in pursuit and chased him back into the house with an umbrella.

An old lady in Hook Road took pity on Monte's sister, Fran, and used to offer her honey sandwiches. The siblings' father, Joseph, died in the 1917 'flu epidemic at the age of 78.

taking sandwiches to his grandfather working in Moon's fields at Hook during school holidays.

There was no water or main drainage at the cottage and Bob snr and Victor had to empty a cesspit. There was no electricity even after the Second World War. At night, it was difficult to see the way across the path over the field from the Hook Road and there was always a danger of stepping in cow's pats. When once, an ambulance was required for Bob's mother, the crew had to carry her across the field. It was possible to drive to the cottage only in the summer when the land had dried out.

In the kitchen was an old coal range and paraffin lamps. Later, illumination was improved with the purchase of tilley and hurricane lamps. These used to have to be pumped vigorously to obtain a glowing mantle.

Sadly, tragedy struck the family when Bob jnr was a boy. His father met with an accident in the area of Middleton Laundry's water tanks and drowned. His father had worked for Middleton's as their cowman. There had been other accidents at the laundry, opened in 1905. As it was being constructed, its founder was involved in an accident which led to him having to wear a silver plate in his skull.

The laundry's gardens were beautiful with snowdrops in springtime. Sheets would be hung up in the drying fields which stretched down to the farms.

Bob jnr recalled the locality still having a distinctly rural flavour. Almost opposite was Brook Farm where Edgar Ford lived. "He used to grow large dahlias with paper bags over them to protect them from frost." Edgar's daughter, Myrtle Richards was still living locally at Warren Drive North, Tolworth, in 2001. Before Herne Road was built it was known as Hookhearne Common. Near to the foot of Herne Road was a smallholding with pigs, kept by 'Bubbles' Chatfield.

"The Verona Drive area used to be a rose nursery after the war, run by Diggers. Hook Cycles — as it became known — was next door, the first shop going up in the parade of shops. Sometimes, in the 1950s, on the bypass, there were trotting races with these chariots.

"Our doctor was Dr McNeill. He was a very kind man and had sweets on the counter for the children. He used to make up the medicines on the premises." Dr Mcneill's premises were at Ravenshurst, a house which used to stand at 64 Hook Road.

Seabreeze Cottage, Hook Road, opposite Haycroft Road, was the home of Joseph Broad in the 1890s. He ran a small coal merchant's in Brook Road, next to the evangelical church. In 1906, Mrs Mary Selfe is listed as its occupant. There is some suggestion that the cottage was redeveloped as Maythorne's Laundry early in the 20th century. John Selfe, a Surbiton Hill landowner, who got into heated disputes with his business colleagues, and his daughter, Hariette, lived at next-door Southborough Hill, now a shopping parade. Mr Selfe died in 1899; made bankrupt by legal wrangles. Naughty boys would haunt the bedridden Miss Selfe in her old age and dress up as ghosts at night and make wailing sounds. She died in 1934 aged 83 and is buried in the family grave next to St Paul's Church, Hook.

Some houses and cottages in Hook and Southborough and their earlier names

Present day location **original name/s**

Hook Road east side

1 Hook Road/Gate House flats..............Gate House/toll collector's home (demolished)
3 Hook Road/Maypole Motors..........................Evans, chemist/part of Maypole Motors
5&7 Hook Road/Maypole Motors...................Malvern Lodge Grange and coach house
9 Hook Road/Malvern Court flats......................................Malvern Lodge (demolished)
11 Hook Road/Midhurst Court.....................................Gardens of Holmbury (Cottage)
13 Hook Road/Midhurst Court..........St David's Villa/Holmbury (Cottage) (built c1870)
15 Hook Road..Devon Villa, (built c1870)
17 Hook Road ....Egerton Villa/Glenholm (built c1870)
19 Hook Road.Yew Tree House......Hook Villa/Hook Road Villa/ Mayfield (demolished)
21 Hook Road..Yew Tree House......................Westfield (built c1865 demolished c1980)
23 Hook Road..Yew Tree House.....Bramley (Guest House) (built c1878 demolished1980)
25 Hook Road...Tarn Lodge/ The Hollies (built c1878)
27-39 area of Hook Road.......Beechcroft and Embleton (6-beds and billiard room, demolished)
45 Hook Road.........Dr J McNeill's (1904) Lynton/ formerly 39 Hook Road (built1904)
47 Hook Road......................................Lynmouth/formerly 41 Hook Road (Edwardian)
49 Hook Road.....................................Inglestone/formerly 43 Hook Road (Edwardian)
51 Hook Road....................................Watersmeet/formerly 45 Hook Road (Edwardian)
53 Hook Road......................Ranmoor/Hindhead/formerly 47 Hook Road (Edwardian)
55 Hook Road...................................Ditton Dene/formerly 49 Hook Road (Edwardian)
57 Hook Road...Milverton/formerly 51 Hook Road (Edwardian)
59 Hook Road..Melinda/formerly 53 Hook Road (Edwardian)
61 Hook Road..Dirleton/formerly 55 Hook Road (Edwardian)
63 Hook Road..Orielton/formerly 57 Hook Road (Edwardian)
65 Hook Road.....................................Vale House/formerly 59 Hook Road (Edwardian)
67 Hook Road...plot of land alongside brook

Here is Vale Road South

69 Hook Road.....Surrey View/Clwyd/Cheshire's grocer's/dairy at rear (built pre-1870)
71 Hook Road, dental surgery......Heatherville/Fairview/butcher/greengrocer (built pre-1870)
73 Hook Road, Ashmore Works...Cook's yard
75/75a Hook Road/Michael de Carle hairdresser....Vale Cottage/formerly 71 Hook Road
77 Hook Road...Elladale/formerly 73 Hook Road
79 Hook Road........2 Vale Terrace/ironmonger/Seaward, shoe repairer/formerly 75 Hook Road
81 Hook Road/Airgraph Carriers....3 Vale Terrace/Ashby's grocer's; formerly 77 Hook Road
83 Hook Road...............4 Vale Terrace, formerly 79 Hook Road/ Turners, shoe repairers

Here is Vale Road North

Verona Drive area................the (H)arbour/Field Cottage/Middleton's laundry/Droitwich (all gone)
Verona Drive..Stickley's field/wartime allotments/Diggers rose nursery
137 Hook Road, Motorite..Hook Cycles (constructed 1930s)
137-151 Hook Road.....shops parade including Hook Road PO/Tip Top Cafe/Penn's newsagent's
Site of parade 137-151.....Echo Villa & Southborough Hill, 135 Hook Road (demolished 1930s)
Site of parade 137-151 (and former field near rear of Bankfield)..........................The hut; piggery
169 Hook Road Comax Security.......................Enfield House/Hook Road Post Office/domestic appliances dealer/Michael Noon estate agents
171 Hook Road/Bankfield......Bankfield/potter's/bank/record shop/Star Hire Coaches/Conway
r/o 171 Hook Road.................Stickley's yard, horse-drawn haulage contractors/coal merchant's
Hook Road/Hewden tool hire (opposite Gladstone Road)...Sea Breeze Cottage/Maythorn Laundry
Southborough School.................... Haycroft Cottage/ 'the hut', grazing meadows for cattle, horses

Here is Hook Underpass/Kingston bypass

Ace Parade/Elmcroft Drive..Haycroft house, and lodge (demolished 1930s)
205 Hook Road...Brockett/General and Municipal Workers Union offices
207 Hook Road...Pelham House & Pelham Lodge/Southernhay
Flower gardens Hook Road...Pelham's orchard and grazing for sheep
233 Hook Road.........................Guildables Cottage or Guildables (demolished) Clifton (built 1932)
235 Hook Road..... ....Belvedere (along with Clifton, built in grounds of Cissendune, 1932)
237 Hook Road, Hooklands Court...Cissendune (demolished c1971)
239 Hook Road, Heasleigh ....No change
241 Hook Road, Hillview...Hill View (1890s)
243 Hook Road..Hillside (1890s)
245 Hook Road ("Hillrise")..Hillrise
247 Hook Road..Norfolk Villa
249, 249a, 251, 251a Hook Road..........site of The Bungalow (built 1892 demolished 1970s)
Clyde Cottage 253 Hook Road...Clyde Cottage (Victorian)

What's in a name? Nos 4-10 and 16-24 Gladstone Road, Hook, in 2001. They were originally known as 1-9 Alderstone Cottages in the 1880s but by 1901 were listed as Ross Cottages. No 4 is today called Pink Cottage.

The Hawthorns and St Quentin, opposite Hook Parish Hall - pulled down in the 1970s.

255 Hook Road.....................site of bungalow and Erica (built 1930s, demolished late 1970s)
McDonough Close.....................The Hawthorns'/259 Hook Road (demolished late 1970s)
257 Hook Road................Meadows/ St Quentin/261 Hook Road (demolished late 1970s)
The North Star at Hook...possibly Lamb and Star/ North Star
273 Hook Road..1 Fenten Vean Villas
275 Hook Road..2 Fenten Vean Villas

Hook Road west side

Here is Ditton Road, Hook Road, Southborough Road cross roads

The Maypole public house..................old Maypole (demolished 1904)/2-6 Hook Road
4&6 Hook Road.......two cottages vicinity of Maypole garden, car park (gone by 1913)
8 Hook Road, Maypole Surgery....... Les Rosiers (built by 1896) Formerly 4 Hook Road
10 Hook Road....................................Middlecot (built by 1891) Formerly 6 Hook Road
12 Hook Road........Southborough Rise/Fircroft (built by 1891) Formerly 8 Hook Road
14 Hook Road ....Bel Air/Wyvenhoe (Formerly 10 Hook Road, built c1905)
16 Hook Road ....Beechdene (Formerly 12 Hook Road, built c1905)
18 Hook Road................Derrynane (one half of Beresford, built 1902; formerly No14)
20 Hook Road..Beresford/Surgery of Dr Richard Mowll & Dr Richard A Mowll (1903-)
The Shrubbery flats 22 Hook Road........the old Shrubbery house (demolished c1930)
Ash Tree Close flats....................Land around Westernhay, 32 Hook Road (demolished)
36 Hook Road...Fairfield or Fairfields (built prior to 1870)
38 Hook Road.......................Fairfield/Southborough Villa/Sungate (built prior to 1870)
42 Hook Road..Coach house (probably for Kirby family)
St Bernard's House. No 54........Southborough Lodge/St Bernard's School (demolished)
56 Hook Road....1 Southborough Terrace/Stormont/earlier 36 Hook Road (late 1850s)
58 Hook Road..............2 Southborough Terrace/Normanshurst/formerly 38 Hook Road
60 Hook Road........................3 Southborough Terrace/Netley/formerly 40 Hook Road
62 Hook Road........................4 Southborough Terrace/Shirley/formerly 42 Hook Road
The Clifton flats 64 Hook Road.....Ravenshurst/Dr McNeill's surgery (Victorian; demolished)
68 Hook Road...Firholm (late Victorian)
70 Hook Road...Rotha (late Victorian)
Warwick Court 72 Hook Road.......Copsham Lodge/Accarsane (Victorian, demolished)
Edward Pinner Court sheltered accommodation..1&2 Brook Farm Cottages (mid-Vic.)
Golf shop, cnr of Brook Road/132 Hook Road.....................Laurel House (built 1870s)
Kareena Cafe etc in parade.(134-140 Hook Road..................St Mary's Villas, built 1883
Brook House, 142&144.................................1&2 Sefton Villas/Linch Villa (built c1870)
Bookmakers, 154 Hook Road.....Gladstone House/Hook PO & public telephone/Al's kitchen
164&166 Hook Road (164 Chessington Motorcycles)... 1&2 Southborough Cottages (built 1860s)
168 Hook Road, Chessington Motorcycles....Southborough Coffee Rooms/The Haven
170 Hook Road, Brock's Insurance agent...... Southborough Coffee Rooms/The Haven
172 Hook Road, DIY shop.............................Crossley House/Lawrence's, the butcher's
174 Hook Road Ormonde Joinery.........the old Southborough Arms (built about 1870)
176 Hook Road, Spirit of Beauty.............Northampton House (Aggas boots and shoes)
178 Hook Road...Bradford House
180 Hook Road Roofing Supplies.........Southborough Stores/formerly 150 Hook Road
182 Hook Road Green Fingers Hydroponics....5 Hook Rd/Seymour's/Woodwards/newsagents
Hook Underpass..Haycroft Farm and agricultural labourers' cottages

Vale Road South

New residential development.......Nos 1-19 Vale Road South (built c1881, demolished 1970s)

Vale Road North

1-11 Vale Road North..Cottages always numbered, built c1900

Haycroft Road (formerly Southborough Road)

2 Haycroft Road...1 Surbiton Cottages (built c1873)
4 Haycroft Road...2 Surbiton Cottages
6 Haycroft Road...3 Surbiton Cottages
8-16 Haycroft Road...1-5 Crowsley or Crossley Cottages
18-24 Haycroft Road..4-1 South West Cottages
26-28 Haycroft Road...1&2 Williams Cottages
7&9 Haycroft Road...2&1 Winsgrove or Winsgrave Cottages
11-27 Haycroft Road...9-1 Hunt's Cottages

Gladstone Road

4-10&16-24 Gladstone Road......1-9 Alderstone Cotts/1-9 Ross Cottages (late Victorian)
12&14 Gladstone Road........................Farmer's Cottages(?)/1&2 Hope Cottages (Victorian)
26-32 Gladstone Road..South View
19&21 Gladstone Road...Walton Cottages (built circa 1863)
23-31 Gladstone Road.....................................1-5 Hornsey Cottages (Victorian, demolished)

Old 'Backy' track rear of Haycroft Road

Garages area, left hand-side of lower track.............possibly site of humble farmer's cottages

Brook Road (formerly St James Road, Southborough)

14&16 Brook Road.....................1&2 Woodland Cottages, St James Road, Southborough
18&20 Brook Road..........................1&2 Leigh Cottages, St James Road, Southborough
22&24 Brook Road..........................1&2 Kenley Cottages St James Road, Southborough
26&28 Brook Road..not ascertained
11 Brook Road...Lynne Cottage
13 Brook Road..Clare Cottages (Victorian)
15-21 Brook Road...North View
Farm building next to Hook Evangelical Church...possibly Selfe's Cottage/Penn's store
Property on corner of Hook and Brook Road...................................land at Brook Farm

The Cricketers

FREDERICK and Annie Boswell were publicans at the Cricketers public house from 1936-1960.

They took over as licencees when the new building replaced an older pub of the same name on the site. Mr Boswell died in 1960 and his widow moved.

In the picture *(left)* can be seen the lanterns outside bearing the words 'saloon', 'private' and 'public' bars. The door in the middle without a lantern led to the 'bottle and jug' — off-licence. Next to the public bar is the entrance to the gents toilet. In those days patrons had to go outside the pub to get to the gents but, thoughtfully, the ladies' toilet was inside. The hanging pub sign showed men playing cricket.

On Christmas Eve, sometimes the couple's young grandson, Roger Smith, would stay over.

He recalled: "I would be told to go to bed and get to sleep because Father Christmas would be coming later. But I couldn't possibly sleep it was so noisy in the bar with all the singing. Sometimes I would creep downstairs to look at what was going on and I could hardly see people because the smoke was as thick as a fog."

The saloon bar was on the left, the private on the the left of the centre, and the public bar, right.

The Cricketers, Clayton Road, in 1960 with Yew Tree Cottage on the right.

Fred and Annie Boswell.

Haycroft — house with 39 acres

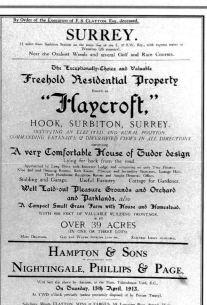

Haycroft, pulled down in the 1930s.

THE impressive Haycroft stood on the site of Elmcroft Drive and Ace Parade. Built in 1860 for John and Emily Clayton, its estate included a lodge, cottage and farm, and extended to 39 acres. It was constructed for the Clayton family — remembered in Clayton Road. They were a family of London solicitors and passionately cared for Hook and Surbiton, performing countless good deeds. The philanthropic activities were continued by sons Francis and Charles. Constance Helder, a relative who lived at Haycroft, married a grandson of the painter John Constable. Francis died in 1912.

Living in style: The drawing room of Haycroft.

More familiar faces in Hook

Retired policeman Alan Buller, born 1938, has lived most of his adult life at Somerset Avenue, Hook, where he is a dahlia-growing celebrity. He even has a species named after him.

Chessington Motorcycles was founded at North Parade in 1964 by Barry Foster. Peter Forsdick (above) bought the business in 1970. It has traded from No 166 Hook Road since 1965.

Mrs Pat Thacker (above) of 43 Somerset Avenue and her team of helpers have made tons of marmalade, pickles and pies to boost St Paul's Church funds over the past decade.

Gone: Guildables Cottage (left) and Cissendune.

One of the many vanished villas

MANY of Hook's old family houses have gone and in their place, modern flats and maisonettes have emerged. On the site of Hooklands Court, 237 Hook Road, a house called Cissendune stood. It was built in the Edwardian era and was home to English sheepdog breeder Charles Winstone, whose family were leather goods manufacturers. He moved into Cissendune in 1915 from Douglas Road, Tolworth. He and his wife, Lydia, had six children. Sons Bill and George were keen 1st Hook scouts. Next to Cissendune was an old cottage, Guildables. It was pulled down and in 1932, Nos 233 and 235, Clifton and Belvedere, were put up. George's widow, Viv, still lived at Clifton in 2001.

About the author

MARK Davison spent the first 21 years of his life in Hook and attended St Paul's School, Hook, and Rivermead School, Kingston, before joining the Kingston Borough News. Although he later moved to Reigate to work on the Surrey Mirror, he retains a keen interest in the history of Hook, Chessington and the surrounding area and has made numerous friends in the district as a result of his research for the Remembered Series of books he has written.

Enid Blyton's daughters Gillian and Imogen with author Mark Davison.

APART from Thomas Hardy, Hook has another famous literary link. As extensively detailed in the companion book, Hook Remembered, children's author Enid Blyton lived at Southernhay, 207 Hook Road from 1920-4 and wrote her first book there. In May 2001, Blyton's daughters, Gillian Baverstock, left, and Imogen Smallwood, met Mark Davison at a Blyton conference and were presented with copies of Hook Remembered. Imogen said afterwards: "Enid's diary indicates how well life at Southernhay suited her and how different and independent her life was back then in the early 1920s."

Tolworth County Secondary Boys' School, (Tolworth Central) Fullers Way North, in July 1948.